W9-DGB-390

COCKTAILS AND HORS D'OEUVRES

A COLLECTION OF CARIBBEAN CHARTER YACHT CONCOCTIONS

Publisher and Editor	Capt. Jan Robinson
Associate Publisher	Waverly H. Robinson
Title by	F. Marion Meginnis
Artist	Raid Ahmad
Cover Illustration	Pat Anderson

To order additional copies of **SIP TO SHORE**
or a *free* catalog, please call
1-800-338-6072

SHIP TO SHORE, INC.

10500 Mt. Holly Road
Charlotte, NC 28214-9219
Phone 704-394-2433 : Fax 704-392-4777
e-mails: CapJan@aol.com
CapJan@perigee.net

P.O. Box 10898
St. Thomas, U.S. Virgin Islands, 00801
Phone/Fax 340-775-6295

SIP TO SHORE

Copyright 1983 by Ship to Shore, Inc

All Rights Reserved
No part of this book may be reproduced in any form or by any
means without prior permission from the publisher.

First printing: September, 1986
Second printing: April, 1988
Third printing: August, 1990
Fourth printing: September, 1993
Fifth printing: November, 1997

ACKNOWLEDGEMENT

Special thanks to all the Charter Yacht Captains
and Chefs who contributed their treasured
cocktail and hors d'oeuvre recipes

Printed in the United States of America

ISBN 0-9612686-2-X

FOREWORD

An outstanding dining experience requires both knowledge and planning. **SIP TO SHORE** provides the guidance and information needed to insure success in the first step - - cocktails and hors d'oeuvre. These two words carry special meaning. The word cocktail is derived from the eighteenth century slang term for a "docked tail", first applied to a horse of mixed breed and then to a nag on a race course. A combined allusion to the society in which drinks are popular and the notion of mixed breeding must have led to the word being applied to alcoholic recipes.

The first cocktails originated in England at the height of the Victorian era. Many cocktails were being made by the end of the century and some of the names are still being used. Coolers, cobblers, cups, daisies, fixes, flips, juleps, nogs, punches, rickeys, sangarees, slings, and smashes all suggest the hilarious nature of those gentleman's origins of some of the mixes.

An hors d'oeuvre is a delicacy served before a meal as an appetizer. It is unusual, extraordinary, and exciting so to stimulate enthusiam for what is to follow.

SIP TO SHORE is a true collection of cocktails and hor d'oeuvre. It includes alcoholic, non-alcoholic, and deliciously diet concoctions. **SIP TO SHORE** recipes are fast and fabulous. The cocktails suggest glass and serving sizes while the hors d'oeuvre recipes offer preparation and cooking times. All recipes include helpful hints and personal notes from their creators.

The primary contributors of **SIP TO SHORE** are Caribbean Charter Yacht Captains and Chefs, who have many years of experience in meeting the needs of discriminating guests.

When planning a dining experience either aboard or ashore, the drinks and appetizers must match your guests likes and be served in a manner that meets the occasion. It is a critical element that demands attention.

The choice is yours. BON VOYAGE!

TABLE OF CONTENTS

* This symbol denotes a cocktail that can be alcoholic or non-alcoholic.

\+ This symbol denotes a cocktail that is nonalcoholic and deliciously diet.

Cocktails

GLASSWARE

Goblet

Old Fashioned

Champagne Flute

Fancy

Liqueur Pousse - cafe

Cocktail

Tulip

Glass Mug

Lager

Whiskey Tumbler

Collins

Balloon

Highball

Brandy Snifter

Champagne Saucer

BLACK VELVET

A St. Paddy's Day Tradition!

Glass: Champagne Flute
Serves: 1

Captain: Richard George
Yacht: Emerald Lady

**1 part dark beer
(Guinness Stout)**

**1 part champagne,
or to taste**

Tilt the chilled glass and pour the stout slowly in. Then fill the glass with champagne.

CHA CHA

Happy Feet!

Glass: Champagne Flute
Serves: 1

Chef: Jane Glancy
Yacht: Graciet

Champagne, chilled

Chambord

Pour a small amount of chambord into a champagne glass. Fill with chilled champagne.

CHAMPAGNE FRAMBOISE

A Lovely Cocktail!

Glass: Champagne Flute
Serves: 8

Chef: Carole W. Manto
Yacht: Drumbeat

**2 pints fresh raspberries
or strawberries
1-2 tsp. Framboise liqueur
per glass (Chambord)**

**1 bottle champagne, chilled
8 long stem glasses, chilled**

Remove stems from berries and freeze 4-5 hours or overnight. Fill glasses with champagne. Add 1-2 tsp. Framboise. Drop in 3 or 4 raspberries, or 1 or 2 strawberries, depending on the size. *Looks and tastes wonderful!*

ELKE SPECIAL

"Woof!"

Glass: Champagne Flute
Serves: 1

Chef: Jan Robinson
Yacht: Vanity

Twist of orange peel
1 lump sugar

2 dashes bitters
Champagne, well chilled

Put a large twist of orange peel into champagne glass. Add 1 lump sugar and 2 dashes bitters. Fill with well chilled champagne and stir! *Woof!*

MINT JULEP COOLER

Definitely Different!

Glass: Collins
Serves: 1

Chef: Marilyn Stenberg
Yacht: Champagne

3-4 sprigs fresh mint
1 tsp. fine white sugar
1 Tblsp. water

Ice
Chilled champagne
GARNISH: orange slice,
            cherry

Crush together in a glass 3-4 sprigs of fresh mint, the sugar, and the water until the sugar is dissolved and the flavors are extracted from the mint. Add some ice and then enough champagne to fill the glass. Decorate with a slice of orange and cherry. *Serve with a straw!*

NANTUCKET RED

This Will Stop You In Your Tracks!

Glass: Tulip
Serves: 1

Chef: Jane Glancy
Yacht: Graciet

Champagne
1 oz. vodka
1 oz. cranberry juice

Ice
GARNISH: lemon wedge

In a tall glass, pour a generous amount of champagne over ice. Add vodka and cranberry juice. Garnish with a lemon wedge.

POINSETTIA

Perfect For The Holiday Season!

Glass: Tulip
Serves: 1

Chef: Jane Dixon
Yacht: Verona Sin Final

1/2 glass champagne,
Ice

1/2 glass cranberry juice,
chilled

Mix and serve over ice.

SILVER LADY

Spine Tingling!

Glass: Tulip
Serves: 1

Captain: Richard George
Yacht: Emerald Lady

1 part champagne, chilled
1 part grapefruit juice
A splash of Cointreau or
triple sec

**GARNISH: cherry, and a
slice of pineapple**

Mix champagne and grapefruit juice one to one in a tall glass. Float Cointreau or triple sec on top. *Garnish with a cherry and a slice of pineapple.*

GUAVA COLADA

A Nice Refreshing Change From Pina Coladas!

Glass: Fancy
Serves: 4

Captain: Pat Rowley
Yacht: Calypso

8 oz. guava juice
4 oz. coconut milk
2 oz. dark rum

2 oz. white rum
Ice

Mix all ingredients in blender at high speed until all ice is blended. Pour into tall glasses. *Serve with straws!*

KIWI COLADA

A New Creation!

Glass: Collins
Serves: 2

Chef: Jan Robinson
Yacht: Vanity

1 1/2 oz. light rum
1 1/2 oz. Midori Liqueur
2 oz. cream of coconut
2 kiwi fruit, peeled
1/4 cup pineapple juice

1 oz. whipping cream
1 1/2 cups small cubes or
   crushed ice
GARNISH: 1 slice kiwi fruit
   1/4 slice of pineapple

Pour ingredients into blender with ice. Blend until smooth. Garnish as shown on cover.

THE KIWI

New Zealanders are proud of their heritage. Two things come into mind, the Kiwi bird and the Kiwi fruit. The now flightless Kiwi is New Zealand's national bird. Dating back 70 million years, this noctural bird is now nearing extinction. The only ones to be found are in captivity. New Zealanders are nicknamed "Kiwis" after this rare bird.

The Kiwi fruit grown in New Zealand was known as the "Chinese Gooseberry" before it became a popular export. Its fuzzy brown covering disguises the lush green melon-tasting inside. Actually it tastes like a cross between a honeydew melon and a strawberry when ripe. The Kiwi fruit, when sliced is a decorative garnish and makes a marvelous "Kiwi Colada". See recipe above.

PEACH-PAPAYA COLADAS

A Whirl Of A Drink!

Glass: Balloon
Serves: 4

Chef: Casey Miller
Yacht: Fancy Free

7 oz. peach nectar
7 oz. papaya nectar
8 oz. rum

1/2 can (6 oz.) cream of
   coconut
Ice

Fill blender with ice and ingredients and whirl.

SOPPYS

The Sweet And Sour Replacement For The Pina Colada

Glass: Fancy
Serves: 6

Chef: Carol Owens
Yacht: Flying Ginny V

1 large or 2 small Soursops,
    peeled and seeded
    (1 1/2-2 cups fruit after
    blending)

6 oz. cream of coconut
6 oz. light or dark rum
4 oz. Coconut Rum
3 cups ice, cubes or chips

Blend or process first 4 ingredients, adding the ice a little at a time until consistency you like is achieved. *Serve with coconut chips hot from your oven for a real Caribbean sundowner treat.*

NOTE: This replaces the pina colada and seems to be even more appreciated, because the Soursap has that "sweet and sour" taste which is not so sweet; neither is it as filling. Initiated in a Tortola beach establishment, the Soppy is a much more "local" taste adventure.

CRANBERRY DELIGHT +

Red Delicious!

Glass: Highball
Serves: 4

Chef: Jan Robinson
Yacht: Vanity

2 cups fresh cranberries, frozen
2 cups tomato juice, chilled
12 oz. diet grapefruit soda, chilled

Ice cubes
GARNISH: sprig of
    parsley

Place frozen cranberries and tomato juice in blender and whirl until mixed. Remove from blender and place in pitcher. Tilt pitcher and add grapefruit soda slowly, pouring down side to prevent too much fizz. Place a few ice cubes in each and pour mixture over ice cubes. Garnish with parsley sprigs and serve.

+Calories 45
  Carbohydrates 10.28 g
  Protein 1.3 g

Fat 0.45 g
Sodium 247.5 mg

CRANBERRY KISS+

Red Lips!

Glass: Champagne Saucer
Serves: 1

Chef: Jan Robinson
Yacht: Vanity

1/2 cup low calorie
   cranberry juice
   cocktail, (no sugar)

3 drops Angostura bitters
1 half-inch sugar cube

Place sugar cube in champagne saucer. Add cranberry juice and Angostura bitters. Let stand for a few minutes until sugar starts to dissolve. Sugar will bubble. Serve immediately.

+Calories 32.5
  Carbohydrates 8.5 g
  Protein 0 g

Fat 0 g
Sodium 12 mg

GAZPACHO +

"From Soup To Drink!"

Glass: Fancy
Serves: 4

Chef: Jan Robinson
Yacht: Vanity

1/4 cup green onions and
   onion tops, cut up
1 cup cucumber, peeled and
   diced
1 cup bell pepper, cut up
1 clove garlic, cut up

2 Tblsp. tarragon vinegar
4 dashes hot pepper sauce
1/2 tsp. salt
1/8 tsp. red food coloring
GARNISH: 4 celery sticks

Place all ingredients except celery sticks in blender and blend throughly. Refrigerate, covered, to chill for several hours before serving. Pour in equal amounts into four chilled glasses. Use celery sticks for swizzles and serve.

+Calories 26.8
  Carbohydrates 6 g
  Protein 1.34 g

Fat 0.16 g
Sodium 1984 mg

JUST PEACHY+

Very Tasty!

Glass: Tulip
Serves: 1

Chef: Jan Robinson
Yacht: Vanity

1 small peach, unpeeled,
   chilled, cut up
1/2 cup plain lowfat
   yogurt

1/2 tsp. sugar or sugar
   substitute
1/16 tsp. powdered ginger
GARNISH: peach slices

Combine all ingredients except garnish in blender and whirl until smooth.
Pour drink into a chilled tulip glass and garnish with a peach slice.

+Calories 112
   Carbohydrates 17.25 g
   Protein 6.9 g

Fat 2.2 g
Sodium 64.55

MANGO MANIA+

For The Diet Conscious!

Glass: Collins
Serves: 4

Chef: Jan Robinson
Yacht: Vanity

1 cup fresh mango chunks,
   chilled
3 tsp. lime juice,
   unstrained and chilled

1 1/2 cups strawberries, fresh
   sliced and chilled
12 oz. diet gingerale, chilled

Put mango, lime juice, and strawberries in blender and whirl until smooth.
Tilt blender and gradually pour gingerale down side to avoid too much fizz.
Pour into glasses and serve.

+Calories 48
   Carbohydrates 11.95g
   Protein 0.67g

Fat 0.43g
Sodium 3.37mg

MANGO MEDLEY+

Make Your Orange Peel!

Glass: Collins
Serves: 4

Chef: Jan Robinson
Yacht: Vanity

1 cup watermelon chunks,
   chilled
1/2 cup mango nectar,
   chilled

1/4 cup fresh orange juice,
   unstrained and chilled
Ice cubes

Place watermelon in blender and whirl until smooth. Add mango nectar and orange juice and blend just to mix. Do not overblend. Place a few ice cubes in each glass. Pour mixture over ice cubes and serve.

+Calories 54
  Carbohydrtes 12.8 g
  Protein 0.58 g

Fat 0.4 g
Sodium 1.25 mg

MANGO MYSTERY+

A Hint Of The Tropics!

Glass: Fancy
Serves: 4

Chef: Jan Robinson
Yacht: Vanity

1 cup mango nectar, chilled
1 banana, cut up
1/2 cup fresh orange juice,
   unstrained and chilled

1/4 cup fresh lemon juice,
   unstrained and chilled
12 oz. diet gingerale, chilled
1 1/4 cups crushed ice

Place mango nectar, banana, orange and lemon juices in blender and blend until smooth. Pour into container. Tilt container and gradually pour gingerale down side to avoid too much fizz. Place 1/4 cup crushed ice in each glass. Pour mixture over ice and serve.

+Calories 44
  Carbohydrates 10.7 g
  Protein 0.37 g

Fat 0.09 g
Sodium 0.4 mg

ORANGE CREAM+

A Cool Sensation!

Glass: Champagne Saucer　　　　　　　*Chef: Jan Robinson*
Serves: 4　　　　　　　　　　　　　　*Yacht: Vanity*

1 1/2 cups orange juice,
　unstrained and chilled
1 1/2 cups skim milk
5 drops yellow food
　coloring

1/8 tsp. imitation flavor
　coconut
1/8 tsp. grated orange rind
GARNISH: orange slices

Place all ingredients except garnish in blender and whirl until mixed. Pour mixture into four glasses. Place glasses in freezer until ice crystals start to form. Remove when icy. Garnish each glass with an orange slice and serve.

+Calories 75
　Carbohydrates 14.36 g
　Protein 3.93 g

Fat 0.26 g
Sodium 48.37 mg

PERFECT PAPAYA+

Sweet Treat!

Glass: Fancy　　　　　　　　　　　*Chef: Jan Robinson*
Serves: 3　　　　　　　　　　　　　*Yacht: Vanity*

1 cup fresh papaya chunks,
　chilled
1 Tblsp. fresh lime juice,
　unstrained and chilled
1 cup mango nectar, chilled

2 tsp. sugar or sugar
　substitute
1 cup crushed ice
Ice water
9-12 ice cubes

Place all ingredients except crushed ice, ice water, and ice cubes in blender and whirl until smooth. Stop blender and add crushed ice. Blend until smooth. Add ice water to bring liquid up to 19 ounces. Place 3-4 ice cubes in each glass. Pour mixture in equal amounts over ice cubes in glasses and serve immediately.

+Calories 80
　Carbohydrates 26.1 g
　Protein 0.67 g

Fat 0.43 g
Sodium 3.37 mg

SMOOTHIE+

A Diet Delight!

Glass: Champagne Saucer
Serves: 2

Chef: Jan Robinson
Yacht: Vanity

1 banana, 6 to 7 inches,
   sliced thin
1/2 cup fresh strawberries,
   thinly sliced
1/2 cup plain low fat yogurt

1/4 cup skim milk
1/4 tsp. grated orange peel
1 tsp. sugar or sugar
   substitute
GARNISH: 3 whole
   strawberries, two straws

Place banana and strawberry slices on a cookie sheet in freezer. Remove when frozen and place in blender jar. Add yogurt, skim milk, orange peel, and sugar substitute. Blend until smooth and thick. Pour mixture into three chilled champagne saucers. Garnish with fresh strawberries and two straws. Serve immediately.

+Calories 95
   Carbohydrates 15 g
   Protein 4.7 g

Fat 2.68 g
Sodium 48.41 mg

SUNSET+

Great For Breakfast!

Glass: Fancy
Serves: 1

Chef: Jan Robinson
Yacht: Vanity

3 oz. orange juice, unstrained
   and chilled
3 oz. tomato juice, chilled
1/8 tsp. dried garden mint

Few drops red food
   coloring
2-3 ice cubes
GARNISH: sprig of mint

Place all ingredients except garnish and ice cubes in blender and whirl. Remove and let stand for 3 minutes. Strain and pour over ice cubes in a fancy glass. Garnish with mint sprig and serve.

+Calories 56
   Carbohydrates 12.48 g
   Protein 1.27 g

Fat 0.25 g
Sodium 182.25 mg

GOOMBAY SMASH
What a party !

Glass: Collins
Serves: 1

Chef: Jan Robinson
Yacht: Vanity

1-1/4 oz. rum (dark or gold)
3/4 oz. coconut rum
3 oz. pineapple juice
1/2 oz. lemon juice

dash of simple syrup (see
page 108)
or
dash of Grenadine

Shake well with cracked ice. Serve in a tall glass. Garnish with cherry and piece of pineapple.
A speciality drink of the Bahamas. Thank you Carleton !

BAHAMA MAMA
Green Shutters Special

Glass: Highball
Serves: 1

Chef: Jan Robinson
Yacht: Vanity

3/4 oz. dark rum
1/2 oz. Nassau Royale
or
1/4 oz. Grand Marnier
1/4 oz. Cointreau

2 oz. orange juice
1 dash Angostura Bitters
1/2 oz. Grenadine
1/4 oz. lemon juice

Shake with cracked ice. Serve in a tall glass. Garnish with an orange slice and a cherry.

THE PUSSER'S PAIN KILLER
Secret Formula

Glass: Collins
Serves: 1

Chef: Charles Tobias
Yacht: Black Fin

1 oz. cream of coconut
1 oz. orange juice
4 oz. pineapple juice

2 oz. Pusser's Rum
GARNISH: freshly grated
nutmeg

Without ice, blend, shake or stir: Pour into a big glass filled with ice and grate fresh nutmeg on top.

FROZEN LIME DAIQUIRI

A Lime Treat!

Glass: Champagne Saucer
Serves: 6

Captain: Jim Carroza
Yacht: Cinderella

1 (6 oz.) can frozen limeade
9 oz. rum
1 oz. cream or
    condensed milk

Ice
GARNISH: lime slices

Put frozen limeade in blender (minus the can). Add 1 1/2 cans rum. Fill blender with ice. Add cream or milk and blend until smooth. *Use lime slices as garnish.*

MANGO DAIQUIRI

Really Tropical!

Glass: Fancy
Serves: 5

Chef: Shannon Webster
Yacht: Chaparral

2 cups fresh mango, peeled
    and chopped
2/3 cup lime juice
1/2 cup dark rum
1/4 cup honey

Dash of triple sec
Ice
GARNISH: maraschino
    cherries, sprigs of mint

Fill the blender with ice. Add all ingredients and blend until mixture is thick and smooth. Pour into tall cocktail glasses and garnish with maraschino cherries and sprigs of mint.

STOWAWAY'S PEACH DAIQUIRI

Nice And Cool!

Glass: Fancy
Makes: 1 pitcher

Chef: Chris Balfour
Yacht: Stowaway

1 (16 oz.) can peaches with
    juice

1 cup rum, or to taste
Ice to fill blender

Blend all ingredients and serve!

VICTORIA'S STRAWBERRY DAIQUIRI

Very Refreshing!

Glass: Fancy
Serves: 4

Chef: Sheila Smith
Yacht: Victorious

**1 (6 oz.) can frozen lime
   juice
1/2 pack (5 oz.) frozen
   strawberries,
   defrosted**

**1 (6oz.) can rum (+1/2 if
   feeling delicate)
Crushed Ice**

Blend all above in liquidizer, add crushed ice, and blend again. *Enjoy!*

CANCUN COFFEE

Best Coffee Drink Ever!

Glass: Mug
Serves: 1

Chef: CJ Burns
Yacht: Grace

**1 lime
Sugar
1/2 oz. kahlua
1/2 oz. anisette (liquorish
   liqueur)**

**1 oz. Bailey's Irish Cream
2 or 3 oz. coffee, brewed
GARNISH: whipped cream**

Wet lip of coffee mug with lime and dip rim in sugar. Pour liqueurs into mug and fill with coffee. Top with whipped cream.

NOTE: This was made for me in Cancun by an aspiring young waiter. Great for a sore throat instead of a hot toddy. Best coffee drink ever. A smooth blend that doesn't taste liquorish!

HOT BUTTERED RUM

Great When Sailing In A Gale!

Glass: Mug　　　　　　　　**⊓P**　　　　　*Chef: Candice Carson*
Serves: 30　　　　　　　　　　　　　　　　*Yacht: Freight Train*

1 lb. butter, softened
1 lb. brown sugar
1 lb. powdered sugar
1 quart vanilla ice cream
1-2 tsp. nutmeg

2 tsp. cinnamon
1 bottle of rum
Boiling water
GARNISH: cinnamon and
　　nutmeg

Cream together butter and sugars. Add ice cream and spices. Freeze this batter and store until needed. To serve, spoon 2 Tblsp. batter into each mug. Add 2 oz. rum and 6 oz. boiling water. Sprinkle with cinnamon or nutmeg on top. *Serve when sailing in Maine or sailing in a gale anywhere.*

PASSAGES PASSION

Ideal For That In Between Time Of Day!

Glass: Mug　　　　　　　　**⊓P**　　　　　　*Chef: Ada Bols*
Serves: 1　　　　　　　　　　　　　　　　*Yascht: Passages*

1 slice of orange
1 slice of apple
1 slice of pear
1 oz. light rum

1 cinnamon stick, long
　　enough to sip through
3/4 cup hearty cider

Place all ingredients in a mug. Cover with the rum. Heat hearty cider til steaming. Pour over fruit. *Serve with a smile. Ideal for that in between time of day when you are caught betwist choices of coffee, tea, or something.*

Hint: To make gourmet coffee, add about 10 grains of salt or 2 to 3 tiny slivers of butter to the grounds in the top of the perculator.

WIND'S END WIND DOWN DRINK

Great For An Easy Dessert!

Glass: Mug   *Chef: Jennifer Morden*
Makes: 6 cups *Yacht: Wind's End*

6 cups decaffeinated coffee,
brewed
2 oz. kahlua
2 oz. Bailey's Irish Cream

Whipping cream
GARNISH: decorator cake
sprinkles, cherries

Combine all, except whipping cream. Pour into mugs. Put whipping cream over all. Sprinkle with decorator cake mint sprinkles. Top with a maraschino cherry. *Serve with sugar cookies.*

ICE CREAM SANDWICH

For the Oreo Cookie Lover!

Glass: Tulip *Chef: CJ Burns*
Serves: 1 *Yacht: Grace*

3 Oreo cookies
1 dip vanilla ice cream
1 oz. creme de cocoa, dark

1 oz. creme de menthe, white
1 cup ice
GARNISH: 1 oreo cookie

Mix all in blender on high speed until smooth. Depending on how hot it is outside, you may need to add 1/2 oz. cream to blend. To make more potent, you can add 1/2 oz. rum. *Serve in a tall glass garnished with an Oreo cookie floating on the top. This will harden as you sip to the last drop! Eat the cookie last! This drink is very filling - is like a dessert.*

NOTE: I started making this drink three years ago while working on Yacht September Morn. After one of these, the owner hired me immediately.

PEACH COOLER

A Great Breakfast Starter!

Glass: Champagne Saucer
Yield: 3 1/2 cups

Chef: Jenn Morden
Yacht: Wind's End

1 pint vanilla ice cream
1 cup fresh or canned
   peach slices
1 (8oz.) carton peach
   yogurt

2/3 cup orange juice
   concentrate
1/3 cup water
GARNISH: sprigs of mint

Combine all ingredients in the container of an electric blender. DO NOT dilute orange juice. Process until smooth. *Garnish with mint sprigs, if desired.*

SMOOTH AND EASY

It's Just That!

Glass: Champagne Saucer
Serves: 4-6

Chef: Jan Robinson
Yacht: Vanity

4 cups chocolate, vanilla, or
   fudge ripple ice cream
6 oz. Bailey's Irish Cream
2 oz. kahlua
2 oz. creme de cacao

2 oz. golden rum
2 oz. white rum
Ice
GARNISH: nutmeg

Fill the blender 2/3 with ice. Add remaining ingredients; blend. Serve in champagne glasses or brandy snifters. *Sprinkle with nutmeg.*

BLUSHING PEACH

Don't Look Away!

Glass: Balloon
Serves: 1

Chef: Jan Robinson
Yacht: Vanity

1 oz. Peach Schnapps
1 oz. strawberry liqueur
1/2 oz. Cream de Cocoa light
4 oz. orange juice

Ice
GARNISH: whole strawberry
   and an orange slice

Pour in shaker with ice - shake! Pour in glass with ice and garnish with a whole strawberry and an orange slice.

CHINOOK I
(The Official Cocktail)

Glass: Cocktail
Serves: 1

Chef: Anne Mallon
Yacht: Chinook I

2 oz. apricot brandy
2 oz. orange juice
2 oz. lemon juice

1/4 oz. sweet vermouth
Ice
GARNISH: orange slices

Mix all ingredients in cocktail shaker, to which ice has been added. Shake if a frothy head is desired. Strain into a cocktail glass. Garnish with a slice of orange. *Great accompanied with almonds, emmental cubes, and Ritz type crackers.*

DEADLY DENISE

Rattle Your Bones!

Glass: Old Fashioned
Serves: 1

Chef: Jan Robinson
Yacht: Vanity

1/2 oz. Peppermint Schnapps
1 oz. Bailey's Irish Cream

1 oz. kahlua
Ice

Pour above ingredients over ice.

EMERALD LADY

A Real Gem Of A Drink!

Glass: Champagne Flute   *Chef: Mardy Array*
Serves: 1   *Yacht: Emerald Lady*

2 oz. unsweetened   1 oz. club soda
   pineapple juice   3 drops green food coloring
1 oz. rum   Ice
1 1/2 oz. Madori liqueur   GARNISH: green
3/4 oz. orange juice   maraschino cherries
1 oz. cream of coconut

Put ingredients in blender, and add 4-5 cubes of ice. Blend until all ice is crushed (slushy). Pour into champagne flute and garnish with maraschino cherries.

NOTE: I have designed this drink for our yacht and hundreds of people have asked for it. This is the first time it's been given out. Enjoy!

FRENCH CONNECTION

An Elegant Finish To An Elegant Dinner!

Glass: Brandy Snifter   *Chef: Lisa Hawkins*
Serves: 1   *Hotel: White Bay Sandcastle*

1/2 oz. Grand Marnier   1/2 oz. Courvoisier

Pour into a brandy snifter and strike match to glass just until heated through.

FUZZY NAVEL

A Peach Of A Drink!

Glass: Cocktail   *Chef: Anne Mallon*
Serves: 1   *Yacht: Chinook I*

1 oz. Peach Tree,   2 oz. orange juice
   (Liqueur) brandy   Ice

Mix together in cocktail shaker to which ice has been added. Strain into cocktail glass.

THE GYPSY

You Put A Spell On Me!

Glass: Liqueur　　　　　　**I**　　　　*Chef: Jan Robinson*
Serves: 1　　　　　　　　　　　　　　*Yacht: Vanity*

1 oz. cognac, chilled　　　　1/2 tsp. instant coffee
Thin slice of lemon　　　　　1/2 tsp. powdered sugar

Pour chilled cognac in glass. Lay the lemon slice on top of the glass.
(Lemon slice should be just a little larger than the rim of the glass.) Spoon
powdered sugar on one half of the lemon and the coffee on the other.
SHOOT - chew the lemon, coffee, and sugar as you drink the cognac. *The
Gypsy does wonderful things to you.*

RUM RUNNER

Caribbean Answer To A Black Russian

Glass: Cocktail　　　　　　**Y**　　　*Captain: Richard George*
Serves: 1　　　　　　　　　　　　　　*Yacht: Emerald Lady*

1 oz. golden rum　　　　　　Ice
2 oz. Tia Maria

Combine one oz. rum with two oz. Tia Maria. *Serve on the rocks with no
garnish.*

SANDCASTLE BLUE LAGOON

Cool As A Ocean Breeze!

Glass: Collins　　　　　　**I**　　　　*Chef: Lisa Hawkins*
Serves: 1　　　　　　　　*Hotel: White Bay Sandcaastle*

1 oz. Blue Curacao　　　　　Juice of one key lime
7-Up or Sprite to fill glass　　Ice

Pour over ice in order above and stir with a swizzle stick.

FROZEN LIME SHERBET MARGARITA

Great On A Hot Afternoon In The Sun!

Glass: Tulip   *Chef: Cathy Heidenreich*
Serves: 2   *Yacht: Mirage*

2 oz. gold tequila
1 1/2 oz. triple sec or
    Cointreau
3 oz. lime mix, bought or
    fresh

2 large scoops lime sherbet
Ice, small cubes or crushed
GARNISH: fresh lime cut in
    wheels

In a blender, place 2 scoops of small cubed or crushed ice, 2 oz. of gold tequila, 1 1/2 oz. triple sec or Cointreau, 3 oz. lime mix and 2 large scoops lime sherbet. Blend well and serve in large tulip glasses. *Garnish with a fresh piece of lime cut in the shape of a wheel and hang it on the glass. A large drinking straw is nice.*

FANTASY'S STRAWBERRY-ORANGE EYE OPENER

A Nice Cool Down In The Afternoon!

Glass: Champagne Saucer   *Chef: D Stetson*
Serves: 4   *Yacht: Fantasy*

1/2 cup milk
1 Tblsp. sugar
1 (10 oz.) package frozen
    strawberries, thawed

2 cups orange juice
About 2 cups ice cubes
GARNISH: fresh strawberries,
    orange wedges

Combine the first 4 ingredients in container of an electric blender and process until smooth. Gradually add ice and process until mixture reaches a desired consistency. *Garnish each serving with a stawberry and orange wedge, if desired.*

MELON FIZZ

No Seeds In This One!

Glass: Fancy
Serves: 4

Chef: Casey Miller
Yacht: Fancy Free

4 cups melon chunks
  (honeydew, watermelon,
  etc.)

1 cup white grape juice
Club soda
Ice

Whirl melon and grape juice in blender. Pour into glasses, fill with ice and club soda.

MORNING PICK- ME- UP

Delicious For Breakfast!

Glass: Tulip
Serves: 4

Chef: Jan Stoughton
Yacht: Mirage

1 ripe banana
1 cup crushed pineapple
  and juice

2 heaping Tblsp. plain yogurt
1 egg
Ice

Put in blender. Fill with ice and mix. Can be sweetened with sugar or honey. Blueberries or strawberries can be added. *Delicious for breakfast with fresh hot Super Muffins. (See Ship To Shore II).*

CRANBERRY PUNCH*

Juice It Up!

Glass: Collins
Makes: 1 gallon

❚

Chef: Jennifer Morden
Yacht: Wind's End

1 (32 oz.) bottle cranberry
    juice
2 1/4 cups pineapple juice
1 1/2 - 2 cups bourbon

1 cup orange juice
1/2 cup lemon juice
7 cups gingerale, chilled
Ice

Combine all ingredients, except gingerale. Chill. Stir in gingerale before serving. Serve over ice.

* Also good without the alcohol.

JELLY NUT RUM PUNCH

Don't Fall Out Of The Tree!

Glass: Jelly Nuts
Serves: 1

Chef: Karen Williams
Yacht: SS Paj

Jelly Nuts
Rum

Ice

I recommend this cocktail as a spontaneous thing to do on a palm-lined beach. First procure your jelly nuts by (a) climbing up a palm tree yourself or (b) finding a small boy and paying him to climb up for you. The latter is recommended. Cut the top off of the nut with a machete if you've one handy, or a sharp knife. Throw in a handful of ice and a shot of rum. Serves one each. Drink straight from the nut.

MARILYN'S RUM PUNCH

A Sun Burnt Body's Delight!

Glass: Collins
Serves: 12-16

Chef: Marilyn Stenberg
Yacht: Champagne

6 oz. brown sugar
1 1/2 cups water
1 bottle dark rum
1 bottle light rum
1 (16 oz.) can orange juice
1 (16 oz.) can pineapple
   juice

1 (16 oz.) can grapefruit juice
Angostira bitters
3 Tblsp. grenadine syrup
1 bottle unsweetened lime
   juice
GARNISH: nutmeg

In your largest pan, boil water and sugar together until sugar is dissolved. Add the rums and the juices. Add enough Angostura bitters to give a good rich color. Stir in 3 Tblsp. grenadine syrup, and then use the lime juice to reach the desired degree of tartness. Some like it sweeter than others. Sprinkle with nutmeg.

NOTE: Bottle the punch - it will keep indefinitely.

MIMOSA HAWAIIAN

Do The Hula!

Glass: Fancy
Makes: 7 cups

Chef: Jennifer Morden
Yacht: Wind's End

1 (12 oz.) can apricot nectar
1 (12 oz.) can pineapple
   juice
1 (6 oz.) can frozen orange
   juice, thawed and
   undiluted

3/4 cup water
1 (25.4 oz.) bottle dry
   white champagne,
   chilled

Combine first four ingredients in a large pitcher.   Stir well.   Stir in champagne immediately before serving.

MY STRIPED TIE

A Great Treat Any Time Of The Day!

Glass: Champagne Saucer
Serves: 8

Chef: Jan Robinson
Yacht: Vanity

2 (12 oz.) can frozen citrus
    juice,(Five Alive)
6 cups milk

1 cup powdered sugar
GARNISH: lime slice

Mix in blender until foamy. Garnish.

PAUL'S PEACHY PUNCH

A Peach Of A Punch!

Glass: Fancy
Serves: 4

Captain: Paul Soule
Yacht: Impervious Cover

2 1/2 oz. light rum
1 1/2 oz. amaretto
1 (8 oz.) can peach slices
    or fresh, if available

3 oz. Half 'n Half or
    light cream
Ice - approx. 2 cups

Put all ingredients in blender. Add as much ice as necessary to fill blender. Blend until creamy.

THE REFRESHER*

A Really Refreshing Drink!

Glass: Old Fashioned
Serves: 6-8

Chef: Carole W Manto
Yacht: Drumbeat

1 (48 oz.) can cranberry
    juice
16 oz. club soda

2 limes, cut into wedges
Ice
2 1/2 cups vodka

Combine all ingredients. Pour into a pitcher of ice and serve.

*It is also good without the vodka.

CARNIVAL PUNCH*

A Caribbean Creation!

Glass: Collins
Serves: 6

Captain: Bob Belschmer
Yacht: Ocean Carnival

1 (46 oz.) can pineapple
    juice
1 (23 oz.) can orange juice
8 oz. guava juice
8 oz. grenadine

Grated nutmeg
1 1/2 oz. rum per glass
GARNISH: orange slices,
    cherries

Shake ingredients. Serve in tall glasses with rum. Sprinkle with grated nutmeg. Add straws and garnish with fresh slices of orange and cherries.

*Equally good without alcohol.

RUM PUNCH
(By The Gallon)

Glass: Fancy
Serves: 12-20

Chef: Laura Greces
Yacht: Mistral

1 (46 oz.) can guava juice
1 (46 oz.) can pineapple juice
1 (16 oz.) can cream of
    coconut
1 (750 ml.) bottle rum

Sugar to taste
Ice
GARNISH: nutmeg, orange
    slices or pineapple
    wedges

Pour ingredients into an empty one gallon pitcher. Shake well. Serve chilled over ice. Garnish with orange slices or pineapple wedges. Sprinkle with nutmeg. *We keep our punch in the ice box on deck so guests can help themselves. A real guest pleaser!*

Note: These two drinks serve with "Boxing Gloves"!!

T.K.O. PUNCH*

It's Sure To Be A Real Knockout!

Glass: Collins
Serves: 6

▌

Chef: Jan Robinson
Yacht: Vanity

1 (23 oz.) can orange juice
1 (15 oz.) can cream of
    coconut
1 (10 oz.) package frozen
    strawberries

1 1/2 Tblsp. lime juice
2 oz. rum per glass
Ice
GARNISH: orange slice

Mix all ingredients except for the rum in a bowl to make the punch. Fill glasses with ice and put the rum in. Then fill the rest of the way with the punch and stir. Garnish.

*Also good without the rum.

TROPICAL FRUIT DRINK

Perfect When The Winds End!

Glass: Collins
Makes: 1 gallon

▌

Chef: Jennifer Morden
Yacht: Wind's End

1 (46 oz.) can pineapple
    juice
1 (15.5 oz.) can cream of
    coconut
7 1/2 cups water

1 (12 oz.) can orange juice,
    thawed and undiluted
GARNISH: pineapple and
    orange slices

Combine all ingredients in a large container. Stir well. Serve chilled. Garnish with pineapple and orange slices.

BETWEEN THE SHEETS

Undercover Agent!

Glass: Cocktail
Serves: 1

Y

Chef: Jan Robinson
Yacht: Vanity

Juice of 1/4 lemon
1/2 oz. brandy
1/2 oz. rum

1/2 oz. triple sec
Ice
GARNISH: lemon twist

Shake with ice and strain into cocktail glass.

BLUE MOUNTAIN COCKTAIL

Crystal Clear!

Glass: Cocktail
Serves: 2

Y

Chef: Charlotte Robinon
Yacht: Excalibur

3 oz. medium-dark rum
1 1/2 oz. vodka
1 1/2 oz. Tia Maria
1/2 cup fresh orange juice

2 Tblsp. lime juice, freshly
    drained
3-4 ice cubes
GARNISH: orange slices,
    and lime twists

Combine all ingredients in a mixing glass. Shake vigorously 9 or 10
times. Strain into glasses and serve at once.

CHOCOLATE CHIQUITA

A Little Brown Banana!

Glass: Champagne Saucer
Serves: 2

Y

Captain Bob Belschmer
Yacht: Ocean Carnival

1 1/2 oz. light rum
1 oz. creme de cacao
1 oz. creme de banana
1/2 fresh banana

1/2 oz. chocolate sauce
GARNISH: whipped cream
    and grated chocolate chips

Mix ingredients in blender. Serve in tall glasses with a dollop of whipped
  cream and grated chocolate chips.

CRANANA SLUSH*

An Excellent Afternoon Smoothie!

Glass: Champagne Saucer   *Chef: Liz Thomas*
Serves: 5   *Yacht: Raby Vaucluse*

1 (6oz.) can frozen cranberry   2 Tblsp. lemon juice
   juice concentrate   4 cups ice cubes
3/4 cup light rum   GARNISH: sliced
1 medium banana, sliced   bananas

In a blender, mix the first four ingredients and blend until smooth. Add half of the ice cubes and blend until smooth. Add remaining ice and blend until slushy. Pour into glasses and garnish with sliced bananas, if desired.

*NOTE By omitting the rum and adding 1/2 cup plain yogurt and 2 Tblsp. honey, this becomes an excellent afternoon smoothie!

ISLANDER*

When In The Islands, Do As The Islanders Do!

Glass: Highball   *Chef: Lisa Ferry*
Serves: 1   *Yacht: Memories*

2 oz. rum   Club soda
1/2 oz. triple sec   Squeeze of lemon
Cranberry Juice

In a tall glass over ice, combine rum and triple sec. Fill with cranberry juice and top with club soda. Add a squeeze of lemon.

NOTE: *Without the liquor, we call it a "Virgin Islander!"

NEW FASHION OLD FASHION

Limit 2 Drinks!

Glass: Old Fashioned   ▯   *Chef: Margo Muckey*
Serves: 1   *Yacht: Tuff*

1 orange slice	1 tsp. bitters
1 maraschino cherry	2 oz. golden rum
1 packet Equal or 1 tsp.	Ice
sugar substitute	Splash of soda
1 tsp. cherry juice	GARNISH: orange slice

Place one orange slice and cherry in bottom of glass. Mash to a pulp with a wooden spoon. Add Equal, cherry juice, bitters, and rum. Stir. Add ice and a splash of soda. Garnish with an orange slice.

NOTE: Equal dissolves better and leaves no bitter taste.

SIMPLE MAI TAI

Quick and Easy!

Glass: Old Fashioned   ▯   *Chef: D Stetson*
Serves: 1 to many   *Yacht: Fantasy*

1 small lime	1/2 oz. dark rum
1/2 tsp. simple sugar syrup	Crushed ice
1/2 tsp. orange curacao	GARNISH: a pineapple slice
2 1/2 oz. light rum	

Squeeze juice of lime on to crushed ice in glass and add other ingredients. Stir to mix. Garnish with a pineapple slice. For serving many, multiply by the number of servings, and make in a large pitcher reserving 1/2 oz. of the dark rum to float on top of each drink.

HINT: Give your glassware the "cold sholder" by placing wet glass in the freezer or by burying them in shaved ice until they are frosty white.

SKIPPER'S SPECIAL

Skip Around The Deck!

Glass: Old Fashioned
Serves: 2

Captain: Harry Newton
Yacht: Once Upon A Time

3 oz. rum
1 oz. triple sec
Splash of lime juice

4 oz. tonic water
Ice
GARNISH: lime twist

Mix all ingredients together and serve over ice with a twist of lime.

STOWAWAY'S SPECIAL

Hidden Treasure!

Glass: Old Fashioned
Serves: 1

Chef: Chris Balfour
Yacht: Stowaway

3/4 oz. lime juice
3/4 oz. sugar syrup
2 oz. pineapple juice
1 oz. orange juice
1 3/4 oz. rum

1/2 oz. Rumona (pimento
   liqueur)
Ice
GARNISH: orange slice and
   a cherry

Shake and serve over ice. Garnish with an orange slice and a cherry.

STRAWBERRY FIELDS

A Run Through The Berry Patch!

Glass: Fancy
Serves: 4

Chef: Jan Stoughton
Yacht: Mirage

1 pint fresh strawberries or
    1 (10 oz.) frozen
    strawberries in syrup
1 cup pineapple juice, to
    taste
2 1/2 oz. cream of coconut
    to taste
Ice

4 oz. golden rum or light
    rum with a generous
    splash of kahlua or
    Grand Marnier
GARNISH: strawberries,
    pineapple slices or
    coconut flakes

Put ingredients in blender. Fill with ice. Blend. Garnish with strawberries, pineapple slices, or sprinkle with coconut flakes.

A TINY PUNCH

It Will Knock You Out!

Glass: Cocktail
Serves: 1

Chef: Cathy Heidenreich
Yacht: Mirage

3 oz. golden rum
2 bar spoons simple
    syrup*

Ice
Fresh lime

In a large shaker glass filled with ice, pour in rum, then pour 2 bar spoons of simple syrup over the ice and squeeze a piece of fresh lime. Shake well and strain into a small glass that has had a squeeze of fresh lime rubbed around its rim and dropped into the glass. *Sip it chilled and straight up or shoot it with your favorite brew!*

*Simple syrup (sugar water): Dissolve one part white sugar in one part boiling water. Skim for impurities. Keep in a jar in the refrigerator.

TROPICAL BLEND

A Great T.G.I.F. Recipe!

Glass: Collins
Serves: 4

Chef: CJ Burns
Yacht: Grace

2 oz. cream of coconut
4 oz. light rum
3 oz. Midori (green melon
    liqueur)

12 oz. pineapple juice
2 1/2 cups ice
GARNISH: pineapple or
    melon chunks

Add ingredients as listed into blender on high speed until frozen. Garnish with pineapple or melon chunks.

NOTE: The higher the speed, the longer the blending time, the thicker the consistency.

THE HORNY BULL*

Makes You Blow Your Horn!

Glass: Tulip
Serves: 1

Captain: Bligh
Yacht: The Bounty

1 1/2 oz. tequila
3 oz. orange juice
1 oz. prepared lemonade

1/2 oz. grenadine
Ice
GARNISH: orange slice

Place all ingredients in blender and blend until firm. Garnish.

*Excellent without alcohol.

PEAR-A-NOID

Caution!

Glass: Old Fashioned
Serves: 1

Chef: Jan Robinson
Yacht: Vanity

1 1/2 oz. Pear Schnapps
1 1/2 oz. tequila

Ice (optional)

Serve on the rocks or as a shot. *Get pear-a-noid!*

BIEN VENIDOS
(Welcome To My Island)

Glass: Fancy
Serves: 5

Chef: Shannon Webster
Yacht: Chaparral

1 oz. triple sec
1 oz. Galliano
2 oz. vodka
1 oz. creme de cassis
1 oz. creme de cacao
Ice

1 oz. Southern Comfort
3 oz. stawberries
2 oz. orange juice
GARNISH: an orange wheel
    and a cherry

Fill the blender with ice. Add all ingredients listed. Blend until smooth, stopping to stir the mixture as necessary. The consistency should be the same as a frozen daiquiri. Garnish with an orange wheel and a cherry. *Very potent! A great un-winder! A fun recipe invented by a friendly island bartender.*

B 58 SHOT

Cheers To The B58!

Glass: Liqueur
Serves: 1

Chef: Jan Stoughton
Yacht: Mirage

1 oz. kahlua
1 oz. Grand Marnier

1 oz. Bailey's Irish Cream
Golden rum, as floater

Layer the liqueurs into a shot glass by slowly pouring each over the back of a spoon so that they run down the inside of the glass. After pouring the three liqueurs, the B58 is completed with a nice floater of rum. Complete all participants drink.

BUSHWHACKER

Add a shot of rum for some more "whack" in the "bush" !

Glass: Old Fashioned
Serves: 1 or many

Chef: Jan Robinson
Yacht: Vanity

Equal parts of: **Baileys**
Kahlua
Dark Creme de Cocoa
White Creme de Cocoa

Blend with ice and serve, sprinkle with nutmeg.

GLAUCOMA

Guaranteed To Cure Blindness Or To Make You Blind!

Glass: Old Fashioned
Serves: 1

Captain: Richard George
Yacht: Emerald Lady

1 oz. vodka
1 oz. rum
1 oz. gin
1 oz. kahlua

4 oz. lemon juice
1 tsp. sugar
Powdered sugar (optional)
Ice

Combine one ounce: vodka, rum, gin, kahlua to four ounces lemon juice with 1 tsp. sugar. Pour over ice in shaker. Shake well. Strain into glass or (blend in blender). Powdered sugar on rim of glass is optional.

GEORGIA'S NEGRONI

Don't Expect To Join In On This One And Then Cook Dinner!

Glass: Old Fashioned
Serves: 1

Chef: Sheila Smith
Yacht: Victorious

3 oz. Campari
1 oz. vodka
Splash of dry vermouth

Ice
Club soda

Throw all in and mix. *Watch out!*

WHAM!

Slam One Down!

Glass: Cocktail
Serves: 2

Chef: Jan Robinson
Yacht: Vanity

1 oz. rum
1 oz. gin
1 oz. Wild Cherry Brandy
1 Tblsp. orange juice,
   concentrate

Grenadine
1/2 oz. triple sec
1 oz. sour mix
Ice

Pour all ingredients in shaker with ice. Put 2 ice cubes in cocktail glass and strain drink into glass. Serve.

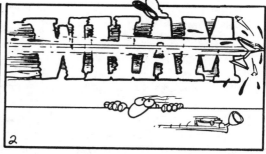

HAIR OF THE DOG*

Great For The Morning After!

Glass: Highball
Serves: 4

Chef: Charlotte Robinson
Yacht: Excalibur

1 (32 oz.) can tomato juice
    or V8
1 (8 oz.) bottle clam juice
Lemon or lime juice,
    to taste
Dash A-1 sauce (optional)
Dash Worcestershire sauce
1 (10 oz.) can beef broth

Celery salt, to taste
Tabasco sauce, to taste
Black pepper, to taste
1 oz. vodka, per glass
Ice
GARNISH: 1 green
    chili per glass

Fill a large bottle or container 2/3 full with tomato or V-8 juice. Pour in beef broth and clam juice proportionally 50-50 til bottle is nearly full. Squeeze in lemon or lime juice. Add a generous dash of Worcestershire sauce, a small dash of A-1, celery salt, tabasco sauce, and black pepper, to taste. Shake well. Pour over vodka and ice in highball glasses and add 1 chili pepper to each glass.

*Also great without the vodka.

MIRAGETTE

All Hands On Deck!

Glass: Old Fashioned
Serves: Many

Chefs: Jan and Cathy
Yacht: Mirage

1 bottle vodka
1 bottle Bailey's Irish
    Cream

Full bucket of ice

To prepare, simply take one full bucket of ice, full bottle of vodka and as many of your favorite cocktail glasses as needed. Get comfortable, fill the glasses with ice and add any proportions of Bailey's and vodka as desired.

NOTE: A "Miragette" is an after dinner crew cocktail to be drunk on the bow of the boat while on charter; preferably under a moonlit sky, at anchor in the Caribbean. The party's over when the bottles are empty, so get yourself to bed because the guests will be up early tomorrow.

RANGGA SLING

Don't Bruise The Gin!

Glass: Fancy
Serves: 1

Chef: Diana Horn
Yacht: Rangga

2 oz. gin
1 oz. Cherry Herring
1/3 oz. Cointreau
1/3 oz. Benedictine
1/3 oz. bitters
2 oz. orange juice

2 oz. pineapple juice
1 oz. lime juice
Ice
GARNISH: orange slice,
   cherry, parasol, and a
   straw

In a shaker full of ice, add all ingredients, except the gin. Shake briskly. Add gin and stir slowly. Don't bruise the gin! Pour into 14 oz. hurricane glass. Garnish with an orange slice, a cherry, a parasol, and a straw.

RECKLESS MARY*

You'll Love Them!

Glass: Collins
Serves: 6

Chef: Mardy Array
Yacht: Emerald Lady

24 oz. V8 juice
7 oz. vodka
3/4 oz. lemon juice
1 drop Worcestershire sauce
1 heaping tsp. horseradish

1/4 tsp. black pepper
1/8 tsp. salt
Ice
GARNISH: celery stalks

Use a 1-quart container, like a tupperware one, marked in ounces. Mix all the ingredients. Pour over ice and add a celery stalk.

NOTE: I make them by the pitcher like this, because no one wants just one.

* Also great without vodka

ROUNDERS RELAXERS

Sit Back And Enjoy!

Glass: Cocktail   *Captain: Tom Miller*
Serves: 1   *Yacht: Fancy Free*

1 oz. vodka   1 oz. lime juice, (Rose's)
1 oz. triple sec   Ice

Put ice cubes in a shaker. Pour in ingredients, shake well, strain. *SHOOT!*

SKIP AND GO NAKED JERRY

Skippidy Do Dah ...

Glass: Collins   *Chef: Jan Robinson*
Serves: 1   *Yacht: Vanity*

1 oz. gin or vodka   Beer
1 oz. sweet and sour mix   Ice

Put the gin and sour mix in a glass over ice. Top with beer. *Cheers!*

STOWAWAY'S RAMOS FIZZ

Great For Hangovers!

Glass: Whisky Tumbler   *Chef: Chris Balfour*
Serves: 2   *Yacht: Stowaway*

1 (6 oz.) can frozen limeade   6 oz. of milk
6 oz. vodka or gin   Ice
1 whole egg

Blend all ingredients. *Very refreshing. Goes well with Eggs Bendict .*

SUNSET WITH A GREEN FLASH

This One Has Flare!

Glass: Champagne Saucer
Serves: 1

Chef: Jennifer Morden
Yacht: Wind's End

2 oz. vodka
1 egg yolk
6 oz. orange juice

1 tsp. sugar
Green tinted sugar
1/2 cup crushed ice

Combine all ingredients (except tinted sugar) with half a cup of crushed ice in a blender. Blend at low speed. Rim cocktail glass with green sugar. Pour drink into a glass. *The orange of the drink and the green sugar makes a great "sunset with a green flash."*

TANGELO FANDANGO

The One That Makes You Dance!

Glass: Whisky Tumbler
Serves: 1

Engineer: Edward Tuleja
Yacht: Rangga

2 oz. gingerale
2 oz. good vodka
Juice of 2 tangelos
1/2 oz. cranberry juice

Ice
GARNISH: the great pumpkin
   or a basket of acorns
 - optional

Into a large glass (with rocks), pour the gingerale, then the vodka, then the fresh squeezed tangelo juice. Give it one swift poke with your largest finger, then slowly add the cranberry juice. *Garnish with the great pumpkin or a basket of acorns - optional!*

MARTINI A LA RUDI

Helping Hands!

Glass: Cocktail   Y   *Chef: Ruth Gardner*
Serves: 1   *Yacht: All Is Best*

1 crystal glass   Lots of gin
Lots of ice   Rudi's right index finger
5 drops dry vermouth   GARNISH: lemon twist

Fill a crystal glass with ice. Add the vermouth. Insert right index finger
into the glass and twirl until the glass is frosted. Pour off excess liquid.
Fill the glass with gin, spinning ice twice. Add lemon twist. *Serve with a
smile!*

THE ULTIMATE MARTINI

Very Inviting!

Glass: Cocktail   Y   *Chef: Jan Robinson*
Serves: 1   *Yacht: Vanity*

2 oz. gin (or vodka), chilled   1 stuffed green olive
Dry vermouth to taste   Ice

Prechill the cocktail glass. Into a mixing glass full of ice cubes, pour
vermouth and gin. Stir well. Strain into a cocktail glass. Garnish with
stuffed olive.

THE MARTINI

Martinis are usually made with about ten to twelve parts gin to one part dry
vermouth. The drink may be served "up" in a stemmed cocktail glass, or
"on the rocks" in an old fashioned glass. You can drop a twist of lemon peel
into the glass or rub the rim with the peel before adding it to the drink. The
most common garnish is a green olive, pitted or stuffed. The martini turns
into a gibson when you add a cocktail onion. A martini must be very cold,
both gin and vermouth should be prechilled in the refrigerator. Stir well
with ice and strain into a prechilled glass.

VALKYRIE KICKER

Kick Your Shoes Off And Enjoy!

Glass: Old Fashioned
Serves: 1

Chef: Jane Dixon
Yacht: Verano Sin Final

1 oz. vodka
1 oz. amaretto

1 oz. Bailey's Irish Cream
Ice

Mix and serve over ice.

BIKINI
(Named After The Bomb)

Glass: Old Fashioned
Serves: 1

Captain: Richard George
Yacht: Emerald Lady

3 oz. bourbon
1 oz. chartreuse
Splash of club soda

Ice
GARNISH: lemon twist

Combine bourbon with chartreuse. Add a spash of club soda and a lemon twist for garnish. Serve on the rocks in a glass. *Limit 2 per guest.*

EASY WHISKEY SOURS

Pucker Up!

Glass: Tulip
Serves: 4

Chef: Sandye Bullard
Yacht: Concrescent

1 (6 oz.) can frozen
   lemonade
6 oz. bourbon, rye, or
   scotch
3 oz. water

Ice, cubed or crushed
GARNISH: maraschino
   cherries lemon or
   orange slices

Mix undiluted lemonade and an equal amount of liquor in blender. Add 3 oz. water. Run blender just to mix. Pour over ice cubes or crushed ice. Garnish with a cherry and a fruit slice.

NOTE: The number of servings depends on the size of the can of frozen lemonade used. A 6 oz. can yields 4 ample drinks and a little of this goes a long way.

FLUTE, FLUTE, FLUTE

A Perfect End To A Long, Hard, Hot Day In Paradise!

Glass: Old Fashioned　　　　　　　　*Captain: Rik Rensselaer*
Serves: 1　　　　　　　　　　　　　　*Yacht: Flute*

2 oz. bourbon　　　　　　　**Ice**
2 oz. amaretto

Pour over ice. Mix. Serve. *It's also fondly known as a "Bye, Bye".*

GINGERIFRIC

Cuts The Salt Taste After A Snorkle On The Reef!

Glass: Coliins　　　　　　　　　*Chef: Lisa Hawkins*
Serves: 1　　　　　　*Hotel: White Bay Sandcastle*

1 oz. green ginger wine　　　**Juice of one key lime**
　　(Stone's)　　　　　　　　**Ice**
7-Up or Sprite to fill glass

Pour over ice in order above and stir with swizzle stick. *A very refreshing drink!*

"NEW YORK, NEW YORK"

A New Version Of The "Manhattan" With Quite A Kick!

Glass: Cocktail　　　　　　　　*Chef: Anne Mallon*
Serves: 1　　　　　　　　　　　*Yacht: Chinook I*

1/2 oz. rye whiskey　　　　　**Ice**
1/2 oz. sweet red vermouth　**GARNISH: a cherry**
Dash of grenadine

Stir ingredients in a mixing glass over ice. Strain into a cocktail glass. Garnish with a cherry.

HOMEMADE IRISH CREAM

A Bailey's Irish Cream Substitute!

Glass: Old Fashioned
Serves: 4-6

Chef: Sandye Bullard
Yacht: Concrescent

1 cup Irish whiskey
1 (14 oz.) can sweetened
   condensed milk
4 eggs, slightly beaten
2 Tblsp. vanilla extract

2 Tblsp. chocolate extract
1 Tblsp. coconut extract
1 Tblsp. powdered espresso
   or coffee
Ice

Blend all ingredients together in blender or food processor. Refrigerate 12-16 hours before serving to allow flavors to mellow. *Serve over ice.*

NOTE: In places where Bailey's Irish Cream is expensive like in the states--or people don't have it with them, the Homemade Irish Cream is fantastic and even richer than Bailey's. Try it out and I think you'll agree.

OLD FASHIONED EGG NOG

A Christmas Favorite!

Glass: Tulip
Serves: 4

Chef: Anne Malllon
Yacht: Chinook I

12 eggs, separated
2 cups sugar
1 quart milk
1 pint heavy cream

1/2 cup rum
1 pint rye whiskey
GARNISH: freshly grated
   nutmeg

Separate eggs. Beat yolks and whites separately. Beat whites until frothy. Add 1 cup sugar to yolks and 1 cup sugar to whites. Beat again. Combine eggs/sugar together. Add milk, cream, rum, and whiskey. Serve in cups or 6 oz. glasses with freshly grated nutmeg as garnish.

NOTE: Chill 2-12 hours. The longer it chills, the stronger it gets. I often make it the night before.

STUFF THE GOOSE
(By Dan Murphy)

Glass: A Big One   *Chef: Jan Robinson*
Serves: Many   *Yacht: Vanity*

1 goose, plucked   **2 cups hard cider**
Cornbread stuffing   **2 bottles Irish Whisky**

Stuff the goose with cornbread stuffing and 2 cups hard cider. Baste every 5 minutes for 12 hours with Irish Whiskey. *Garbage the goose and drink the gravy!*

Hors d'oeuvre

BANG!

Preparation Time: 5 minutes   *Chef: Diana Horn*
Cooking Time: 15-20 minutes   *Yacht: Rangga*
Serves: 6-8

1 block Edam cheese, peele   **Sherry**
1-2 cloves garlic, minced   **10 canned biscuits**

Preheat oven to 350 degrees Fahrenheit. In a 9-inch glass pie dish, sprinkle minced garlic over bottom. Add enough sherry to cover bottom. Place peeled Edam in centre and surround with biscuits and bake in a moderate oven (350) for 15-20 minutes or until biscuits are golden and the cheese is melted. Serve as is. Pull apart and spread melted cheese on hot biscuits.

BAKED BRIE TOAST

Preparation Time: 10 minutes   *Chef: Dawn Drell*
Cooking Time: 3-5 minutes   *Yacht: Helios*
Serves: 4

1 loaf French bread   **Pommery mustard**
1/4 cup butter   **1/2 lb. Brie cheese**

Slice the bread. Butter each slice, follow with mustard and top with Brie. Broil for 3-5 minutes or until Brie is melted and hot. *Serve immediately.*

CLASSIC BAKED BRIE

Preparation Time: 5 minutes   *Chef: Jane Dixon*
Cooking Time: 2 minutes   *Yacht: Verano Sin Final*
Microwave: 10 seconds
Serves: 4-6

1/2 lb. Brie cheese,   **1 cup almonds, sliced**
    roon temperature   **1 loaf hot crusty French**
1/2 cup butter   **bread**

Place butter and almonds in a small saucepan. Melt butter and heat until butter is frothy. Place Brie on microwave-safe serving platter and "nuke" 10 seconds until soft to the touch. Do not melt. Pour butter and almonds over. *Serve with hot bread and napkins! This is messy!*

CAMEMBERT A LA VIERGE

Preparation Time: 10 minutes
Cooking Time: 10 minutes
Serves: 6

Chef: Kim Turk
Yacht: Antipodes

7-inch round Camembert
   cheese
1 egg, beaten

1 loaf French bread
Butter or margarine
1/2 cup breadcrumbs, to coat

Dip cheese in beaten egg. Then coat in bread crumbs. Saute until golden brown about 10 minutes or crunchy outside and creamy inside. *Serve with fresh French loaf.*

STUFFED CAMEMBERT

Preparation Time: 10 minutes
Cooking Time: 15 minutes
Serves: 6

Chef: Kim Turk
Yacht: Antipodes

7-inch round Camembert
   cheese
1/2 cup chutney
6 slices bacon, cooked and
   crumbled

1 clove garlic, minced
1 tsp. chives
1 cup walnuts, chopped
Crackers (I prefer Carr's)

Preheat oven to 350 degrees Fahrenheit. Cut top off Camembert and set aside. Make a small hollow in cheese. Cube the cheese you cut out. Mix the cubed cheese and the other ingredients. Then fill the hollow and replace the top. Bake for about 15 minutes at 350 or until creamy. *Serve with crackers.*

stuffed Camembert

CHEESE BALL

Preparation Time: 30 minutes   *Chef: Dorie Devnew*
Makes: 2 large balls or 4 small balls   *Yacht: Winji*

1 (8 oz.) package cream
   cheese, softened
1 lb. hoop cheese, mild,
   grated
1 lb. New York sharp
   cheese, grated
2 cloves garlic, minced

1 Tblsp. dry onion soup
   mix, (Liptons)
1/4 cup mayonnaise
1/4 tsp. Worcestershire
   sauce
1/4 tsp. tabasco sauce
1 cup chopped nuts

Mix garlic, soup mix, mayonnaise, Worcestershire sauce, and tabasco together. Add cheeses and mix well. Form 2 balls. Roll in chopped pecans. Serve with your favorite crackers.

NOTE: Cheese balls may be made ahead and frozen.

CHEESE FONDU

Preparation Time: 15 minutes   *Chef: Fiona Baldrey*
Cooking Time: 15 minutes   *Yacht: Promenade*
Serves: 10

1 clove garlic
2 wine glasses dry white
   wine
1 lb. Gruyere cheese, grated
1 tsp. flour

1/2 wine glass Kirsh
1/2 oz. butter
Cubed French bread
   (for serving)

Rub the inside of a pan with garlic. Mix together wine and Gruyere cheese. Place in the pan over medium heat. Stir continually until a thick mixture is obtained. Blend flour with Kirsch. Stir into mixture to bind. Add the butter. *Serve immediately with French bread cut into cubes and forks!*

HINT: Grate old bits and pieces of cheese, then mix them together with some spices. Use this to make a cheese ball or use on top of spaghetti or lasagna. Also delicious on top of a tossed salad.

SESAME CHEESE SQUARES

Preparation Time: 10 minutes
Cooking Time: 10 minutes
Serves: 6-8

Chef: Anne Mallon
Yacht: Chinook I

1 lb. cheese, Swiss,
Emmental,or Jarlberg
type, cubed
1/2 cup bread crumbs

1/4-1/3 cup sesame seeds
2 eggs, beaten
Oil for frying

Heat oil in frying pan. Cut cheese into cubes. Mix bread crumbs and sesame seeds together. Dip cheese cubes in beaten eggs, then into bread crumbs and sesame seed mixture. Repeat dipping process again to coat cheese well. Drop in hot oil. Fry quickly to crisp, but not melt the cheese. *Serve with toothpicks.*

CREAM CHEESE AND CRAB

Preparation Time: 15 minutes
Serves: 6

Chef: Donna Keller
Yacht: Adela

1 (8 oz.) package cream
cheese, softened
1/4 cup ketchup and
horseradish, mixed
to taste

1 (6 1/2 oz.) can white
crab meat
Lemon wedges

Spread cream cheese on platter. Cream cheese can be spread in shapes - anchor, fish, sailboat, etc. Then spread ketchup/horseradish mixture on cream cheese. Cover-with crabmeat and sprinkle with a little lemon. *Surround with your favorite crackers.*

STUFFED CREAM CHEESE ROLL

Preparation Time: 15 minutes   *Chef: Jane Dixon*
Serves: 6-8   *Yacht: Verano Sin Final*

1 (8 oz.) package cream cheese
1 (4 1/2 oz.) can deviled ham
1 (4 oz.) can mild green
    chilies, chopped
1 Tblsp. horseradish
Dash of Worcestershire sauce

A couple of dashes of
    tabasco
Chunky Taco sauce, mild
GARNISH: chives, shredded
    Cheddar hot peppers,
    black olives

Roll out cream cheese between two layers of plastic wrap to 1/2 inch thickness. Mix the rest of the ingredients well, except taco sauce and place in the center of cream cheese. Roll up and place on platter. Cover with taco sauce. Garnish with chives, shredded Cheddar, hot peppers and black olives. *Serve with crackers.*

NOTE: This recipe is Alex Kinney's. She was the cook on Tropic Bird for years. Alex passed away this past summer and I submit this recipe in memory of her.

STUFFED GOUDA

Preparation Time: 30 minutes   *Chef: Jacklyn Johnson Rabinowitz*
Chilling Time: 2 hours   *Yacht: Endless Summer II*
Serves: 8

1 (16 oz. or 2- 8 oz.) Gouda
    cheese
1/2 cup dark beer
2 tsp. mustard, Dijon or
    Pommery

1 Tblsp. fresh dill, chopped
    or 1 tsp. dried dillweed
1/4 cup butter, cut in pieces
GARNISH: sprigs of dill

Cut 1/2-inch off the top of the cheese and discard. Hollow out the cheese leaving the shell intact. Cut cheese in small chunks and place in a blender or processor. Add the remaining ingredients and whirl until smooth. Stuff shell with cheese mixture. Makes 2 cups of spread. Garnish with sprigs of dill. *Serve with crackers.*

ROB'S ROLL

Preparation Time: 10 minutes
Chilling Time: 30 minutes
Serves: 4

Chef: Jan Robinson
Yacht: Vanity

1 (8 oz.) package cream
   cheese, softened
1/4 tsp. tabasco sauce
1/3 cup stuffed green
   olive, chopped

1/4 cup black olives, chopped
1 Tblsp. onion, finely
   chopped
1 bunch of parsley, chopped

In medium mixing bowl, combine cream cheese with green and black olives, onions, and tabasco. Mix thoroughly. Set cheese mixture in refrigerator for about 15 minutes to harden slightly for easier handling. Shape cheese mixture into ball. Roll in chopped parsley to coat well. Return to refrigerator. Chill 15 to 20 minutes or until serving time. *Serve with assorted crackers.*

NOTE: Cheese mixture can also be thinned with sour cream or milk to serve as a dip. Use parsley as a garnish.

MACADAMIA CHEESE BALLS

Preparation Time: 10 minutes
Chilling Time: 20 minutes
Serves: 8-10

Chef: Jan Robinson
Yacht: Vanity

8 oz. cream cheese
4 oz. Bleu cheese
8 oz. sharp Cheddar cheese,
   grated

1/4 cup peach chutney,
   chopped
1 cup macadamia nuts, finely
   chopped or substitute
   walnuts

Soften cheeses and blend together . Add chutney and chill a little. Shape (about 1 tsp.) into small balls. Roll in nuts and chill until serving. Insert a toothpick in each ball and serve with fruit wedges.

MACADAMIA CHEESE DROPS

Preparation Time: 15 minutes
Cooking Time: 8 minutes
Makes: 48

Chef: Jan Robinson
Yacht: Vanity

1/4 cup margarine, softened
1 cup buttermilk biscuit mix
1 egg, slightly beaten
1 cup Macadamia nuts,
    coarsely chopped

1/2 cup sharp Cheddar
    cheese, shredded
Red pepper, to taste

Preheat oven to 400 degrees Fahrenheit. Blend margarine and biscuit mix until it is in coarse crumbs. Stir in egg, nuts, cheese. Drop by a teaspoon onto greased cookie sheet. Bake 8 minutes.

HOT ARTICHOKE DIP

Preparation Time: 10 minutes
Cooking Time: 30 minutes
Serves: 6-8

Chef: Jane Dixon
Yacht: Verano Sin Final

1 (6 oz.) jar marinated
    artichoke hearts
1 (6 oz.) can unmarinated
    artichokes
A couple dashes of tabasco

6 Tblsp. mayonaise
Salt and pepper to taste
1 (4 oz.) can mild green
    chilies

Preheat oven to 350 degrees Fahrenheit. Drain and chop artichokes and chilies. Mix in remaining ingredients. Bake at 350 until warm (about 30 minutes), stirring occasionally. *Serve warm with crackers.*

NOTE: Could also be heated in microwave.

POTATO PEELS WITH CAVIAR DIP

Preparation Time: 15 minutes   *Chef: Jan Robinson*
Cooking Time: 30 minutes   *Yacht: Vanity*
Serves: 8-10

POTATO PEELS:

2 Tblsp. unsalted   Peelings from 6 scrubbed
   butter,melted   baking potatoes, 1/4 inch
1/2 tsp. seasoning salt   thick; (leave some potato
1/4 tsp. pepper   on peel) 3/4 inch wide,
                    2 inches long

Preheat oven to 425 degrees Fahrenheit. In a bowl, combine melted butter, seasoning salt, and pepper. Brush peels wtih mixture. Arrange skin side down on a buttered baking sheet. Bake in a preheated 425 degree oven 15-20 minutes until lightly browned. Turn them and bake 10-15 minutes more or till golden brown.

CAVIAR DIP:

6 oz. jar Caviar   1 Tblsp. minced onion
   (Red or Black)

Gently mix ingredients together. Chill for about 1 hour. Serve with Potato peels.

BEAN DIP

Preparation Time: 10 minutes   *Chef: Kimberly Foote*
Cooking Time: 15 minutes   *Yacht: Oklahoma Crude II*
Serves: 6

1 (10 oz.) can chili beans   Spices of choice
1 cup Cheddar cheese, grated   GARNISH: parsley
Worcestershire sauce

Preheat oven to 400 degrees Fahrenheit. Drain oil from beans. In an oven-proof dish, layer beans, grated cheese, Worcestershire sauce and spices. Repeat. Bake at 400 for 15 minutes until cheese is crispy. Garnish with parsley. *Serve with taco chips.*

DEEP BLEU CHEESE DIP

Preparation Time: 15-20 minutes   *Chef: Jeanne Felton*
Chilling Time: 2 hours   *Yacht: Prego*
Serves: 6-8

4 oz. Bleu cheese, room   8 oz. mayonnaise
   temperature   6 oz. Half n' Half or
4 oz. cream cheese, room   light cream
   temperature

Reserve half of Bleu cheese. Combine remainder with cream cheese. Mix thoroughly and add mayonnaise and mix. Gradually pour in cream. Crumble remaining Bleu cheese and stir in. This makes a chunky dip, which thickens as it sets. Chill 2 hours to enhance flavor. If too thick, add small amounts of cream. *Serve with crinkle-cut carrots, cucumbers, or zucchini slices, etc. whatever is available and a favorite.*

NOTE: This recipe is nice in a hollowed out loaf of round bread.

HINT: When whipping cream, use confectioners sugar in place of granulated sugar. The cream is fluffier and holds up longer.

BRUSSEL SPROUTS WITH COCKTAIL DIP

Preparation Time: 15 minutes   *Chef: Anne Mallon*
Chilling Time: 1 hour   *Yacht: Chinook I*
Serves: 6

2 (16) cans brussel sprouts,   1-2 Tblsp. catsup
    cooked   1-2 Tblsp. horseradish
4 oz. mayonnaise

Drain brussel sprouts, then rinse in cold water. Cut out "core" of each
sprout. Mash cores together in bowl. Add mayonnaise, catsup, and
horseradish, to taste. This resembles cocktail sauce in appearance and taste.
Spoon into brussel sprouts. Chill 1 hour and serve.

NOTE: Brussel sprouts can also be served without stuffing them, just
drain brussel sprouts and serve with the cocktail sauce - *Dip in and enjoy!*

HOT CRAB DIP

Preparation Time: 10 minutes   *Chef: Jane Dixon*
Cooking Time: 30 minutes   *Yacht: Verano Sin Final*
Serves: 6-8

1 (7 1/2 oz.) can crabmeat   2 Tblsp. onion, chopped
1 (8 oz.) package cream   1/4 tsp. salt
    cheese, room temperature   Dash of pepper
1/2 Tblsp. horseradish

Preheat oven to 350 degrees Fahrenheit. Mix all ingredients well. Bake at
350 about 30 minutes until warm throughout, stirring occasionally. *Serve
with crackers.*

NOTE: Could also be heated in microwave.

CRAB IMPERIAL DIP

Preparation Time: 15 minutes   Chef: *Charlotte Robinson*
Cooking Time: 15 minutes   Yacht : *Excalibur*
Serves: 6-8

1/2 cup green pepper, minced
2 Tblsp. unsalted butter
12 oz. cream cheese, softened
1/4 cup mayonnaise
Capers, minced and drained
Dry white wine or sherry
1 Tblsp. horseradish, drained

2 tsp. Worcestershire sauce
1 tsp. lemon rind, minced
Tabasco sauce
Salt, to taste
Black pepper
3/4 lb. crab meat
Breadcrumbs

Preheat oven to 350 degrees Fahrenheit. In a skillet, cook green pepper in butter over moderate heat for 3 minutes. In a glass or ceramic bowl, combine green peppers with cream cheese, mayonnaise, capers, wine, horeradish, Worcestershire sauce, lemon rind, tabasco and seasonings. Fold in crab meat. Transfer to 1 quart baking dish. Sprinkle with breadcrumbs and bake til bubbly. *Serve with crackers.*

NOTE: I like to stuff mushrooms with this.

HOT CRABMEAT COCKTAIL DIP

Preparation Time: 10 minutes   Chef: *Sandye Bullard*
Serves: Many   Yacht: *Concrescent*

3 (8 oz.) packages
    cream cheese
1/2 cup mayonnaise
2/3 cup dry white wine
Garlic powder or garlic salt

2 tsp. prepared mustard
Onion powder
2 tsp. confectioners sugar
3 (or 4) 10 3/4 oz. cans
    crabmeat

Cream cheese, mayonnaise, wine, then all the seasonings. Pick over crabmeat for shells. Fold into mayonnaise mixture by hand. *Do not use a beater.* Heat in a double boiler and serve hot. Serve with crackers or toasted rounds of French bread or party rye.

CURRY DIP

Preparation Time: 10 minutes   *Chef: Barbie Haworth*
Chilling Time: 1 hour   *Yacht: Ann-Marie II*
Makes: 2 cups

1 (8 oz.) package cream   **1/2 tsp. dry mustard**
   cheese, softened   **1/2 cup chutney, chopped**
2 tsp. curry powder   **1/2 cup almonds, chopped**

Mix all ingredients thoroughly and refrigerate. *Serve with a variety of fresh vegetables or tortilla chips.*

NOTE: This stores for a long time.

GAYLE'S FAVOURITE

Preparation Time: 10 minutes   *Chef: Jan Robinson*
Chilling Time: 30 minutes   *Yacht: Vanity*
Serves: 8-10

2 (8 oz.) packages cream   **1 (7 1/2 oz.) can crabmeat,**
   cheese, softened   **drained**
1/4 cup green onions,   **1/2 lemon**
   chopped   **1 bottle cocktail sauce**
2 Tblsp. soy sauce   **seasoned with horseradish**
                                   or use "hot" Cajun style
                                   sauce.

Mix cream cheese, green onions, and soy sauce together and spread in a glass bowl. Add 1 bottle of cocktail sauce and spread over cream cheese mixture evenly. Squeeze $^1/_2$ lemon over drained crabmeat and sprinkle over cocktail sauce. Chill 30 minutes or several hours. *Serve with triscuits. Looks and tastes great!*

NOTE: If no time to chill, use as a dip.

HOT DIP WITH SLICED APPLES

Preparation Time: 10 minutes   *Chef: Jan Robinson*
Cooking Time: 10 minutes   *Yacht: Vanity*
Serves: 8-10

6 slices bacon, cooked
8 oz. cream cheese
2 cups Cheddar cheese, grated
6 Tblsp. cream
1 tsp. Worcestershire sauce

1/4 tsp. dry mustard
1/4 tsp. onion powder
4 dashes tabasco sauce
Wedges of red and green
    apples, unpeeled

Crumble bacon. Melt cream cheese in double boiler. Stir in grated cheese and cream. Add remaining ingredients. Add crumbled bacon in melted cheese mixture. Serve in chafing dish to keep warm. Serve with alternating slices of Granny Smith and Red Delicious apples.

NOTE: Great taste and eye appeal. Easy to make ahead and reheat.

ORIENTAL DIP

Preparation Time: 10 minutes   *Chef: Barbara Stride*
Chilling Time: 1/2 hour   *Yacht: All Is Best*
Serves: 8

1/2 bunch parsley
Handful of green onions,
    chopped
Handful of water chestnuts,
    chopped
2 Tblsp. soy sauce

1-inch piece fresh ginger,
    crushed
1 cup mayonnaise
1-1/2 cups sour cream
Freshly ground black pepper
GARNISH: Sprig of parsley

Combine all above ingredients, blend well. Chill for 1/2 hour. Garnish with a sprig of parsley. *Serve with crackers or a variety of crisp vegetables e.g carrots, green onions, green and red peppers, mushrooms, cauliflower, celery.*

PRAIRIE FIRE DIP

Preparation Time: 20 minutes
Cooking Time: 10 minutes
Serves: 6

Chef: Liz Thomas
Yacht: Raby Vaucluse

1 (10 3/4 oz.) can
   enchilada dip
1/2 cup Provolone cheese,
   shredded

1/4 cup milk
2 Tblsp. butter or margarine
Corn chips, tortilla chips,
   or vegetable dippers

In saucepan, combine enchilada dip, cheese, milk, and butter or margarine. Heat and stir for 5-10 minutes or until hot. Transfer dip to a serving bowl and serve immediately. If possible, serve in fondu pot, keeping it warm. *Surround with chips and vegetables.*

SHOE PEG DIP

Preparation Time: 10 minutes
Marinating Time: 1 hour
Serves: 8-10

Chef: Jan Robinson
Yacht: Vanity

1 (16 oz.) can shoe peg corn
1 medium tomato, chopped
1/2 green pepper,chopped
1 jalapeno pepper, chopped

2 Tblsp. mayonnaise
Lemon pepper
Whole wheat wafers

Drain corn and add remaining ingredients including a generous amount of lemon pepper. Let stand at least 1 hour before serving. *Serve with whole wheat wafers.*

NOTE: Also delicious served as a salad with beef.

After eating Prairie Fire Dip !!

SMOKY SALMON DIP

Preparation Time: 5 minutes　　　　　　　　*Chef: Lisa Ferry*
Chilling Time: 2 hours　　　　　　　　　　*Yacht: Memories*
Serves: 6

1 (7 3/4 oz.) can salmon
1 (8 oz.) package cream
　cheese, softened
1/3 cup onion, finely
　chopped

1 Tblsp. lemon juice
2-3 tsp. liquid smoke,
　to taste
3 dashes hot pepper sauce
GARNISH: bed of lettuce
　and tomato wedges

Combine all ingredients by hand or in a blender. Form into a ball and chill for 2 hours. *Serve on a bed of lettuce with tomato wedges. Accompany with cocktail pumpernickel bread or your favorite crackers.*

DEVILISHLY GOOD SHRIMP DIP

Preparation Time: 5 minutes　　　　　　　*Chef: Lisa Ferry*
Chilling Time: 1/2 hour　　　　　　　　　　*Yacht: Memories*
Serves: 4

1 (6 1/2 oz.) tin shrimp
1/3 cup Miracle Whip
3 scallions, chopped
2 Tblsp. parsley, chopped
2 stalks celery, finely
　chopped

1 tsp. paprika
4 dashes tabasco
1 Tblsp. Worcestershire
　sauce
1/4 tsp. pepper, freshly
　ground
GARNISH: cucumber rounds

Combine all ingredients. Chill. *Serve in a small glass bowl ringed with cucumber rounds. Accompany with goldfish thins, pumpernickel thins, or your favorite cracker.*

NOTE: Can be expanded and garnished as a salad course at lunch.

HINT: Be imaginative in serving dips.   Hollow-out red cabbages, lemons, oranges, egg plants, red and green peppers, grapefruits or pineapples to make shells. These make lovely bowls.

SPINACH DIP

Preparation Time: 10 minutes   *Chef: Norma Trease*
Chilling Time: 2 hours   *Yacht: Caroline*
Serves: 6

2 (10 oz.) packages spinach,   1 cup sour cream
   chopped, well-drained   1 package Ranch dressing
1 cup mayonnaise   mix
                                            GARNISH: red pepper

Mix all ingredients together well. Chill 2 hours to marry flavors.
Garnish with bottom of a red pepper, cut to resemble a flower. *Serve in
bowl surrounded by taco chips. Very popular!*

TACO DIP

Preparation Time: 10 minutes   *Chef: Wendy Mitchell*
Cooking Time: 30 minutes   *Yacht: Falcon Gentle*
Serves: 6

2 (8 oz.) packages cream   1 cup Cheddar cheese,
   cheese   grated
1 (1 1/4 oz.) package taco   1/2 cup black olives, sliced
   seasoning   Nacho chips
1 (10 oz.) can chili
   without beans

Preheat oven to 350 degrees Fahrenheit. In a baking dish, blend cream
cheese and taco seasoning mix. Pour chili on top. Layer with Cheddar
cheese. Then with sliced black olives. Bake at 350 for 30 minutes.
 Border casserole dish with nacho chips. *Good before a Mexican or Italian
dinner.*

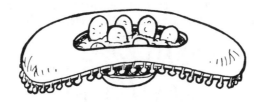

TEX-MEX DIP

Preparation Time: 15 minutes   *Chef: Lisa Hawkins*
Serves: 10   *Hotel: White Bay Sandcastle*

2 cans (16 oz.) refried beans
1/2 cup mayonnaise
2 avocados, medium ripe
Lemon juice
Salt and pepper
1 cup sour cream
1 package taco seasoning
    mix

1 bunch green onions,
    chopped
1 (4.2 oz.) can ripe olives,
    drained and sliced
2 medium tomatoes, chopped
2 cups Cheddar cheese, grated
GARNISH: sour cream and
    shredded lettuce

Spread serving platter or 2-quart casserole with refried beans. Mash avocados and coat with lemon juice, salt and pepper. Spread over beans. Combine sour cream and mayonnaise with taco mix. Spread over avocado. Layer onions, olives and tomatoes. Cover with cheese. Garnish with a big dollop of sour cream and shredded lettuce. *Serve with nacho chips.*

NOTE: Chef Jan Robinson on Yacht Vanity adds 2 Tblsp. Jalapeno peppers after the refried bean layer and 1 (8 oz.) bottle of Picante sauce over the tomato layer.

TZAZIKI

Preparation Time: 5 minutes   *Chef: Sheila Smith*
Chilling Time: 1 hour   *Yacht: Victorious*
Serves: 4-6

1/2 cucumber
1 (4 oz.) carton plain yogurt
Salt and pepper
Paprika

Dash of olive oil
Fresh mint (optional)
2-3 cloves garlic, crushed
Chips of your choice

Finely chop the cucumber or even better, grate the cucumber -depending on how you value your knuckles! Mix all the ingredients together in a bowl. The fresh mint is lovely, but not vital. Refrigerate for 1 hour. *Serve as a dip with chips.*

WATERCRESS DIP

Preparation Time: 10 minutes *Chef: Nan Gee*
Serves : 6-8 *Yacht: Tuff*

2 cups sour cream 2 Tblsp. white horseradish
1 package Hidden Valley 2 Tblsp. watercress, finely
Ranch dressing mix chopped

Mix and chill until ready to serve. *Great with raw vegetables or bagel chips.*

PATE EGGS

Preparation Time: 20-25 minutes *Chef: Dorie Devnew*
Makes: 12 halves *Yacht: Winji*

6 hard cooked eggs 1 Tblsp. butter, creamed
1-1/2 cups liver paste or Salt, to taste
   pate de foie gras GARNISH: seived yolks,
   mayonnaise

Peel and cut eggs in half lengthwise. Fill white halves with pate mixture. Decorate with sieved yolks and mayonnaise mixed together to make a paste and force through a pastry tube. These are extremely rich! *Serve on a platter of Romaine lettuce.*

NOTE: Pour a bit of distilled vinegar in boiling water with eggs. Helps to contain cracked eggs. Also makes eggs easier to peel.

SEAFOOD EGGS

Preparation Time: 20-25 minutes *Chef: Dorie Devnew*
Makes: 12 halves *Yacht: Winji*

1-1/2 cups cold crabmeat, 1-1/2 Tblsp. Russian
   shrimp, or lobster dressing
2 Tblsp. parsley, chopped GARNISH: sieved egg yolk,
1 Tblsp. chives, chopped or sweet gherkin, sliced
6 hard cooked eggs, chilled thin

Cut eggs in half, lengthwise. Reserve egg yolk for garnish. Mix all ingredients and fill the whites, cut lengthwise. Garnish with chopped or sieved egg yolk or thinly sliced sweet gherkin pickle.

ALOHA CRISPS

Preparation Time: 10 minutes   *Chef: Jan Robinson*
Cooking Time: 8-10 minutes   *Yacht: Vanity*
Makes: 16 crisps

1-1/3 cups (13 oz. can)   1/2 lb. (about 8 strips)
   pineapple chunks, drained   bacon, halved

Preheat broiler. Wrap a strip of bacon around each pineapple chunk. Secure with a toothpick. Broil 8-10 minutes until bacon is crisp. *Serve hot!*

CRACKERS 'N FRUIT

Preparation Time: 10 minutes   *Chef: Jan Robinson*
Cooking Time: 5 minutes   *Yacht: Vanity*
Serves: 8-12

1 (8oz.) package cream   2 tsp. triple sec
   cheese, softened   4 doz. multi-shaped crackers
2 Tblsp. orange juice   5-6 cups assorted fresh fruits
1 tsp. ornage rind, grated   (grapes, kiwi,
                                strawberries, etc.)

Preheat oven to 350 degrees Fahrenheit. Mix cream cheese with orange juice, orange rind, and triple sec. Lightly toast crackers in oven. Spread crackers with cream cheese mixture. Cut fruits into various shapes. Decorate tops of crackers with fruit. Makes 4 dozen.

LITTLE SPIDERS

Preparation Time: 10 minutes   *Chef: Georgina Morris*
Cooking Time: 5 minutes   *Yacht: Natasha*
Serves: 6

3 plantains, ripe, but not   Chutney or sweet and
   mushy   sour sauce orany piquant
Flour to coat   tomato-based sauce,
Oil for frying   optional

Grate plantains on large holes of grater. Form into flat patties, and dust in flour with your hands. Lower with a slotted spoon into hot oil. Fry until golden brown. Drain on paper towels and serve with sauces. *Simple and good!*

PINEAPPLE SPECIALTY

Preparation Time: 10 minutes
Chilling Time: 2 hours
Serves: 6

Chef: Liz Thomas
Yacht: Raby Vaucluse

1 (8 oz.) package cream
   cheese, softened
3 Tblsp. pineapple, crushed
1 cup pecans or walnuts,
   chopped

2 Tblsp. green pepper,
   chopped
2 Tblsp. onion, chopped

Mix cream cheese, pineapple, green pepper, onion, and 1/2 cup of chopped nuts. Transfer to a small bowl. Top with remaining 1/2 cup of chopped nuts. Chill for 2 hours. *Serve with an assortment of crackers.*

PLANTAIN CHIPS

Preparation Time: 10 minutes
Cooking Time: 20 minutes
Serves: 4-6

Chef: Sarah Sheets
Yacht: Royono

6 ripe plantains, peeled and
   sliced into rounds

Vegetable oil, for cooking
Salt

Heat oil. Cook plantain rounds in batches until browned on both sides. Drain on paper towels. Sprinkle with salt.

HOT SAUSAGE ROLL

Preparation Time: 10 minutes
Chilling Time: 30 minutes
Cooking Time: 15 minutes
Makes: 3 dozen

Chef: Jan Robinson
Yacht: Vanity

1 package pastry mix

1 lb. sausage, highly
   seasoned

Preheat oven to 375 degrees Fahrenheit. Mix pastry according to directions. Roll out thin and spread with sausage. Roll like a jelly roll. Refrigerate until cold. Slice thin and bake in 375 degree oven until brown. Serve hot. Makes 3 dozen.

CORNED BEEF APPETIZER BALLS

Preparation Time: 10-15 minutes　　　　　　　　　*Chef: Jean Crook*
Chilling Time: 1 hour　　　　　　　　　　　　　　*Yacht: Dileas*
Serves: 10

1 cup Cheddar cheese,
   shredded
4 oz. cream cheese
6 oz. corned beef, shredded
1/4 cup sweet pickle relish
2 tsp. prepared horseradish

1 tsp. Dijon mustard
1 tsp. Worcestershire
   sauce
1/2 tsp. lemon rind, grated
1/2 Tblsp. lemon juice
1/2 cup fresh parsley,
   chopped

In mixing bowl or food processor, blend together cheeses, corned beef, relish, horseradish, mustard, Worcestershire sauce, lemon rind, and lemon juice. Cover and refrigerate for 1 hour or until firm. Shape mixture into 2 balls. Roll each ball in parsley and refrigerate until serving time. Each ball will make 4 or 5 servings. *Serve with crackers or pumpernickel bread.*

PIGMY PIZZAS

Preparation Time: 15 minutes　　　　　　　　*Chef: Jan Robinson*
Cooking Time: 20 minutes　　　　　　　　　　*Yacht: Vanity*
Makes: about 3 dozen

1 package party rye bread
1 (8 oz.) can pizza sauce
1/2 lb. Mozzarella cheese,
   grated

1 lb. seasoned sausage,
   browned and drained
1 (8 oz.) jar Cheese Whiz
Parmesan cheese, grated

Preheat oven to 300 degrees Fahrenheit. Place bread on cookie sheets. Put a teaspoon of pizza sauce on each slice, then cover with other ingredients in order listed. Sprinkle with Parmesan cheese. Bake at 300 degrees for 20 minutes or until browned. *Can be made ahead and frozen.*

KOREAN STYLE BEEF

Preparation Time: 15 minutes　　　　　　　*Chef: Sandye Bullard*
Marinating Time: 6 hours　　　　　　　　　*Yacht: Concrescent*
Cooking Time: 5 minutes
Makes: 15-20

1 1/2 lbs. boneless steak,　　　　　1/8 tsp. pepper
　(sirloin, flank, or round)　　　　1 slice fresh ginger root, 2
Tblsp. vegetable oil　　　　　　　　 finely chopped OR 1/4
1/4 cup onion, minced　　　　　　　　 tsp. ground ginger
1/4 cup soy sauce　　　　　　　　 Bamboo skewers (6" long)
1 large garlic clove,　　　　　　　 1-3 tsp. honey
　minced

Optional: small fresh mushrooms or other vegetables as desired.

Cut steak into very thin slices. Thread meat on bamboo skewers, pushing
skewers in and out of each meat slice as though sewing. In a 9" x 5" loaf
pan, combine all the rest of ingredients (add amount of honey satisfying
sweetness desired). Place skewered meat in marinade turning once to coat
all sides. Cover and refrigerate 6 hours or overnight. Turn occasionally.
When ready to serve, garnish each skewer with optional vegetables.
Preheat broiler or barbeque grill. Broil meat about 2 minutes, basting
with marinade, until evenly browned. Serve hot. Makes 15-20 appetizer
servings.

SAUCISSON SOUL

Preparation Time: 5 minutes　　　　　　　*Chef: Jean Thayer*
Cooking Time: 15 minutes　　　　　　　　　*Yacht: Finesse 60*
Serves: 8

1 lb. smoked sausage　　　　　3 Tblsp. sugar
　(kielbasa)　　　　　　　　　 3 Tblsp. Dijon mustard
3/4 cup white wine

Cut kielbasa into 1-inch slices, then quarter slices. In a large skillet, heat
kielbasa in wine over high heat. Boil rapidly till wine has almost
evaporated and looks syrupy. Add sugar to glaze. Turn off heat and stir in
Dijon mustard. *Serve with toothpicks.*

TARTARE VANITY

Preparation Time: 10 minutes   *Chef: Jan Robinson*
Serves: 8-10   *Yacht: Vanity*

1 1/2 lbs. of the finest cut   1 onion, finely chopped
   lean sirloin or fillet of   2 Tblsp. capers
   beef, freshly ground   Hot buttered toast or
1 egg   Romaine lettuce
Salt and pepper   2 anchovies, optional
                                      GARNISH:hard cooked eggs

Mix all the above ingredients together. Spread about 1/2" thick on hot buttered toast fingers or on Romaine lettuce leaves. Garnish with chopped hard cooked eggs if desired.

TERIYAKI MEATBALLS

Preparation Time: 15 minutes   *Chef: Jan Robinson*
Cooking Time: 20 minutes   *Yacht: Vanity*
Makes: 4 dozen

1 lb. lean ground beef   1 Tblsp. salad oil
1/2 cup onion, chopped   2 tsp. sherry
1/4 cup breadcrumbs   1/2 cup water
1 egg   2 Tblsp. brown sugar
1/2 tsp. salt   1/4 tsp. powdered ginger
1 tsp. pepper   2 tsp. garlic, minced
1/4 cup soy sauce   2 tsp. cornstarch

Combine ground beef, onion, bread crumbs, egg, salt, pepper, and 2 Tblsp. soy sauce. Shape into balls about 1 inch in diameter. Heat oil in skillet. Fry meatballs until lightly browned. Remove from skillet. Combine remaining soy sauce, sherry, water, brown sugar, ginger, garlic, cornstarch. Cook in skillet over low heat until thickened, stirring constantly. Return meatballs to skillet and simmer covered. They freeze well.

NOTE: A faster way is to put meatballs on a cookie sheet and brown in oven at 350 degrees Fahrenheit. Make the sauce in a saucepan and add the meatballs when browned.

THE BEST POPCORN YOU'VE EVER HAD

Preparation Time: 5 minutes   *Chef: Judith Meyers Vegiard*
Cooking Time: 15 minutes   *Yacht: Ruach*
Serves: 6-12

10 oz. unpopped popcorn   Salt, to taste
1/4 lb. butter   Dried parsley, to taste
Garlic powder, to taste   4 oz. Parmesan cheese,
                              grated

Pop popcorn according to package directions. Put in large paper bag. Melt butter. Drizzle butter over popcorn, shaking bag to coat popcorn evenly. Add all other ingredients using the same method. Shake into serving bowl.

NOTE: This serves 6-12 depending on how many true popcorn fanatics you are serving!

HOT RYES , MY WAY

Preparation Time: 15 minutes   *Chef: Barbara Lowe*
Cooking Time: 15 minutes   *Yacht: Tri My Way*
Serves: 8

1 cup Swiss cheese   1 tsp. Worcestershire
1/4 cup cooked bacon,   sauce
    crumbled   1/4 cup mayonnaise
1 (4 1/2 oz.) can olives,   Party bread: rye,
    chopped   pumpernickel, white,
1/4 cup green onion, minced   etc.

Preheat oven to 375 degrees Fahrenheit. Mix together all ingredients except bread. Spread on party bread and bake 375 degrees 10-15 minutes or till browned. *Serve hot!*

NOTE: Chef Jane Dixon of Yacht Verano Sin Final adds 2 Tblsp. Grey Poupon mustard to her mixture. These may be frozen and reheated.

OYSTER CRACKER NIBBLES

Preparation Time: 10-15 minutes   *Chef: Dorie Devnew*
Serves: 6-8   *Yacht: Winji*

1/2 cup oil   1 (1 oz.) package Original
1 tsp. dill weed   Ranch dressing
1/2 tsp. garlic powder   1 box oyster crackers
1 tsp. lemon pepper seasoning

Mill all ingredients together and sprinkle over crackers. Coat well. Pour oil over coated crackers and stir until well mixed.

NOTE: This can be stored in refrigerator for up to 3 weeks - if they last that long!

PINWHEELS

Preparation Time: 15 minutes   *Chef: Barbara Lowe*
Cooking Time: 7-10 minutes   *Yacht: Tri My Way*
Serves: 12

1 package puff pastry filo   Dijon mustard
    dough (2-14 x 18 sheets)   6 slices Swiss cheese,
12 thin slices ham   cut in half

Preheat oven to 425 degrees Fahrenheit. Thaw pastry sheets for 20 minutes. Roll out two 14-inch x 15-inch rectangles. Cut lengthwise into three 5-inch wide strips. Then cut each strip in 1/2 making six 5-inch x 7-inch pieces. Put one slice of ham on each square. Spread with mustard, and top with a slice of cheese. Fold in sides, and roll each rectangle up, jelly-roll style. May be frozen at this point. Cut each roll into 6 slices and place cut side up on a well greased cookie sheet. Bake at 425 degrees Fahrenheit for 7 to 10 minutes or until brown and puffed.

You might need this for Oyster Cracker !!

POTATO LATKES

Preparation Time: 15 minutes   *Chef: Sandye Bullard*
Cooking Time: 10 minutes   *Yacht: Concrescent*
Makes: Lots

2 eggs
1/2 small onion
1 tsp. salt
2 Tblsp. flour
Oil for frying

1/4 tsp. baking powder
3 cups cubed raw pototoes,
    peeled*
Sour cream, at serving time

*NOTE: If doing by hand, do not cube potatoes. Estimate number needed to equal 3 cups grated.

In food processor or blender, put first 5 ingredients and 2 cups potatoes in and mix together, but DO NOT blend to smooth consistency. Add rest of potatoes and blend , being certain mixture retains small bits of potatoes.

If doing by hand: using smallest opening on hand grater, grate whole peeled raw potatoes to obtain 3 cups. Grate onion on smallest opening and add to potatoes plus rest of ingredients except oil and sour cream.

Heat an even coating of oil in pan. Drop mixture by rounded tablespoons into hot oil. Then brown on bottom side, flip and fry second side. When second side is brown, drain on paper toweling. At this point, serve hot with sour cream for dipping or freeze and reheat in oven when ready to serve. Sour cream enhances the taste. Makes lots.

These may sound like a strange thing to serve as an hors d'oeuvre, but they are really good with drinks and are an unusual kind of item.

LOBSTER PATE

Preparation Time: 5 minutes   *Chef: Geli Burrill*
Chilling Time: Overnight   *Yacht: Jolie Brise*
Makes: 2 1/2 cups

1 (8 oz.) package cream
    cheese, softened
1/4 cup dry white wine
1/2 tsp. onion salt
1/2 tsp. seasoned salt

1/8 tsp. dill weed
1-1/2 cups lobster meat,
    finely chopped
GARNISH: parsley sprigs
    and lemon wedges

Beat softened cream cheese and wine until smooth and creamy. Blend in salts and dill. Add lobster. Cover and refrigerate overnight to mellow. Garnish with parsley sprigs and lemon wedges. *Serve with crackers.*

SAMOSAS*

Preparation Time: 45 minutes
Cooking Time: 20-25 minutes
Serves: 8

Chef: Karen Williams
Yacht: SS Paj

PASTRY:
1/2 lb. plain flour
1/2 tsp. salt

4 Tblsp. water
4 Tblsp. vegetable oil

FILLING:
1 lb. potatoes, cooked and
   diced
1 tsp. ground coriander seed
1 onion, finely chopped
1 (6 oz.) package frozen peas
1 tsp. ground cumin
1/4 tsp. cayenne pepper
Oil for deep frying

1 small piece of ginger,
   finely grated
2 Tblsp. lemon juice
1 hot chili or local pepper,
   finely chopped
3 Tblsp. cilantro or
   parsley**

*Samosas are the spicy vegetable pastries sold everywhere on the streets in India.

**Try to find cilantro, a wonderful pungent herb. If you can not, use parsley.

To make pastry, sift flour and salt. Dribble the oil and rub onto mixture until it resembles breadcrumbs. Slowly add water. Make a stiff ball of dough and knead for 5 minutes until smooth. Put aside in refrigerator. Make filling by frying chopped onion in hot oil until brown. Add peas, ginger, hot pepper, cilantro, and add a little water if it looks as though it is drying out. Simmer until peas are cooked. Then add cooked potato, coriander, cumin, cayenne, and lemon juice. Stir to mix and heat through for 3-4 minutes. Roll out pastry into 3-inch rounds. I use a wine glass as a cutter. Lay a teaspoon of filling in each circle, fold in half and seal with water. Flute the edge with a fork. Deep fry in hot oil, until golden brown. *Serve warm with mango chutney.*

SUPER NACHOS

Preparation Time: 20 minutes
Cooking Time: 2 minutes
Serves: 4

Chef: Lisa Ferry
Yacht: Memories

Nacho chips
1 tomato
1 medium onion
1/2 green pepper
1/2 red pepper
1 small jar black olives,
　　sliced (optional)

1 avocado
1/4 cup sour cream
1/2 cup hot taco sauce
1 cup Cheddar cheese
1 cup Fontina cheese or other
　　soft white cheese, grated

Chop tomato and onion. Seed and slice pepper into thin strips. Slice black olives if using. Peel and thinly slice avocado. Layer these ingredients on nacho chips. Top with dollops of sour cream and taco sauce. Sprinkle with a mixture of cheeses and place under broiler til cheese melts. *Serve immediately.*

CHICKEN PATE

Preparation Time: 20 minutes
Cooking Time: 1 hour
Serves: 8

Chef : CJ Burns
Yacht: Grace

1-1/2 lbs. boneless chicken,
　　cooked
3 eggs
1 bunch scallions
Quarter slice of ginger
1 clove garlic
2 Tblsp. peanut oil

2 Tblsp. soy sauce
2 Tblsp. sesame oil
2 Tblsp. sherry or Frangelico
Pinch of salt and pepper
1 cup walnuts, halves
GLAZE: plum sauce

Preheat oven to 350 degrees Fahrenheit. Blend 1/2 chicken, eggs, and onions in a blender. Add all remaining ingredients except walnuts. When well pureed, mix in walnuts by hand, and put in a well oiled loaf pan. Bake for 60-70 minutes at 325. Press walnut halves on top of loaf. Glaze with plum sauce. *Serve sliced with an assortment of fresh fruits: grapes, apples, pears, and cheese and crackers.*

KITTY'S SHRIMP PATE

Preparation Time: 30 minutes
Cooking Time: 10 minutes
Chilling Time: 2 hours
Serves: 4-6

Chef : Charlotte Robinson
Yacht: Excalibur

3 quarts water
1/2 lemon, juice and peel
1 Tblsp. Worcestershire
   sauce
1/2 Tblsp. dried green onion
3 tsp. salt
1/2 tsp. tabasco
1 hard boiled egg, grated
1 Tblsp. small capers
1 1/4 lbs. raw or frozen
   shrimp, shelled and
   deveined

1 cup mayonnaise
2 (3 oz.) packages cream
   cheese, softened
4 tsp. unflavored gelatin
1/3 cup lemon juice, strained
1/4 cup cold water
1 tsp. Worcestershire
   sauce
1/4 tsp. tabasco
1/2 tsp. paprika
1 tsp. onion, juice or
   puree

Combine first 6 ingredients and bring to a boil. Add shrimp and cook til pink. Remove, chop and set aside. Melt gelatin in water. Add remaining ingredients and shrimp and mix well. Pour into 9-inch mayonnaise greased loaf pan or mold. Chill until firm, unmold. *Serve with crackers.*

SARDINE   PATE

Preparation Time: 10 minutes
Chilling Time: 1 hour
Serves: 4

Chef: Fiona Baldrey
Yacht: Promenade

1 (4 -1/4 oz.) can sardines,
   in oil
3 oz. cream cheese
1/4 tsp. Worcestershire sauce
1 tsp. lemon juice

Salt and pepper
1 tsp. green onion,
   finely chopped
GARNISH: lemon slices

Drain the liquid from the sardines and mash with all other ingredients. Press into a pate dish and chill. Garnish with a thin slice of lemon per person. *Serve with hot toast.*

ROSALIND'S CHICKEN LIVER PATE

Preparation Time: 30 minutes   *Chef: Rosalind Rice*
Cooking Time: 10 minutes   *Yacht: Endless Summer II*
Chilling Time: 1-2 hours
Serves: 8-10

1 lb. chicken livers   1 Tblsp. dried thyme
2 medium onions   1 bay leaf
2 small cloves garlic, crushed   Salt and pepper
6 Tblsp. butter   1 Tblsp. sherry
1 Tblsp. parsley, chopped   GARNISH: stuffed green
                                         olive slices

Melt 2 Tblsp. butter. Add onions and crushed garlic. Cook until onions
are soft. Add chicken livers and saute 2-3 minutes. Add herbs and
seasonings, and continue cooking for 4-5 minutes. Discard bay leaf and
place mixture in a blender. Blend until smooth. Melt remaining butter
and stir into pate along with the sherry. Pack into a mound and chill.
Garnish with stuffed green olives slices. *Serve with fingers of toast.*

Fiona Baldrey of Yacht Promenade adds: 1 cup fresh mushrooms sliced
                                        4 slices bacon, chopped
                                        2 Tblsp. whipping cream

Sheila Smith of Yacht Victorious suggests stuffing tomatoes with paste
and baking at 425° for 8-10 minutes

NOTE: If you've never made chicken liver pate because it takes so long,
try this! It's the quickest I've come across.

SNOW PEAS WITH BASIL CREAM SAUCE

Preparation Time: 15- 20 minutes   *Chef: Jean Crook*
Cooking Time: 40-60 seconds   *Yacht: Dileas*
Makes: approx. 40

1/4 lb. snow peas   1 Tblsp. fresh basil,
4 oz. cream cheese   chopped or 1/2 tsp. dried
1 Tblsp. fresh parsley,   1 tsp. lemon juice
    chopped or 1/2 tsp. dried

Blanch snow peas 40-60 seconds until bright green. Refresh under cold
running water. Slit peas open along straight seam. Wrap and refrigerate if
making in advance. Combine cheese, parsley, basil, and lemon juice. Fill
peas with small spoonful of cheese mixture. Arrange decoratively on
platter. For more color, serve with a bowl of cherry tomatoes.

ALEX'S FLUTE

Preparation Time: 5 minutes
Cooking Time: 30-35 minutes
Serves: 6-8

Chef: Lee Ann LaCasa
Yacht: Flute

1 package puff pastry,
   (2-14 x 18 sheets)
1 (8 oz.) package cream
   cheese, softened

1 (8 oz.) package Sea Legs,
   sliced lengthwise
4 Tblsp. soy sauce (approx.)
1 egg, beaten

Preheat oven to 350 degrees Fahrenheit. Remove puff pastry and leave room temperature for about 20 minutes. Gently open pastry and lay flat. Spread 4 oz. softened cream cheese on each to cover. In the center, arrange sea legs in single layer. (About 1/3 of the pastry). Sprinkle 2 Tblsp. soy sauce on each pastry over sea legs. Fold from left and then from right. Brush with beaten egg. Bake on cookie sheet for 30-35 minutes at 350 degrees Fahrenheit until lightly browned and puffed.

NOTE: This is from our little pal Alex Krone. Launched January 3, 1985.

BIMINI PICKLED FISH

Preparation Time: 10 minutes
Curing Time: 3 hours
Serves: 8

Chef: CJ Burns
Yacht: Grace

2 cups raw fish
1/2 cup apple cider vinegar
1 onion, chopped in rings
4-6 whole cloves
Dash tabasco sauce

2 Tblsp. lemon juice
1 Tblsp. sugar
1 tsp. bay leaves, crushed
1 bell pepper, sliced in rings
Salt and pepper, to taste

Cut the fish into bite size pieces. Add all ingredients making sure all the fish pieces are completely covered. Toss every time you pass by. *Serve with diamond toast or French bread toasted with butter, garlic salt, and Parmesan cheese. When charter guests go diving in the afternoon, just clean fish, and fix for afternoon delights. Great when made with dolphin, mahi mahi, or wahoo.*

CAVIAR SURPREME

Preparation Time: 15 minutes
Chilling Time: overnight
Makes: 64 squares

Chef: Barbie Haworth
Yacht: Ann-Marie II

6 hard cooked eggs, chopped
3-4 Tblsp. mayonnaise
   (Helman's)
1 medium red onion, chopped
1 (8 oz.) package cream
   cheese, room temperature

2/3 cup sour cream, room
   temperature
2 small jars black cavier
1/2 sprig fresh parsley,
   chopped

Line bottom of a 8 x 8 pan with waxed paper for easy removal. Combine chopped eggs and mayonnaise. Spread over the bottom of the pan. Sprinkle chopped onion over eggs. Combine cream cheese and sour cream till smooth. Spread over onions. Cover and chill overnight. Before serving, spread on drained caviar and chopped parsley. Remove wax paper from pan gently. Cut in 1-inch squares. *Serve on toasted bread rounds or melba toasts.*

NOTE: Chef Carol Watkins Manto of Yacht Drumbeat usually makes different designs with the red and black caviar such as the "ying and yang" symbol.

NOTE: Chef Sarah Sheets of Yacht Royono combines her hard cooked eggs with melted butter, instead of using mayonnaise.

CRAB PUFFS

Preparation Time: 10 minutes
Cooking Time: 10 minutes
Makes: 50

Chef: Sarah Sheets
Yacht: Royono

3/4 lb. crabmeat
1 cup mayonnaise
1/2 cup scallions, minced

1/4 cup Parmesan cheese
Garlic powder, to taste
Worcestershire sauce, to taste

Mix all ingredients. Spread on melba rounds or Cressca Toasts. Broil until bubbly.

LITTLE LOBSTER QUICHES

Preparation Time: 15 minutes   *Chef: Nan Gee*
Cooking Time: 20 minutes   *Yacht: Tuff*
Makes: 12

1 package Stouffers Lobster   1 egg, slightly beaten
   Newburg   1/2 cup Swiss, Gruyere,
1 (10 oz.) package refrigerated   or Cheddar cheese, grated
   butterflake rolls

Preheat oven to 375 degrees Fahrenheit. Combine thawed lobster with beaten egg, breaking lobster into small pieces. Grease mini muffin tin. Separate each dinner roll in half and press into cups to make shell. Spoon in lobster mixture (about 2 tsp.) Top with cheese and bake at 375 for 20 minutes or until golden. *Serve hot!*

CONCH FRITTERS

Preparation Time: 1 hour   *Chef: Jim Carroza*
Chilling Time: 1 hour   *Yacht: Cinderella*
Cooking Time: 3 minutes
Serves: 2-6

Fresh conch   Sweet red peppers
Fresh lime juice   Hot peppers
Ground pepper   Onion
Tomatoes   Flour
Carrots   Beer
Celery   Oil for frying

Quantities are not important! Clean and dice conch. Add lime juice, ground pepper and other vegetables, diced. Chill. This can be served as a conch salad. For fritters, add flour and small amounts of beer to bind everything together. Deep fry until brown. Serve with tartar sauce and cold beer.

CONCH PUPUS*
(Conk Pooh Poohs)

Preparation Time: 30 minutes   *Chef: Sylvia Dabney*
Cooking Time: 10 minutes   *Yacht: Native Sun*

2 conchs, fillet with orange   1/2 cup Parmesan cheese
   and black skin removed,   1/2 cup processed Italian
   use only white meat   bread crumbs
1/2 cup butter, melted   Butter for frying

*NOTE: Pupus, (pooh poohs) is the Hawaiian name for hors d'oeuvres.

Pound conch fillets with meat pounder until paper then. Preference dictates - thicker conch will be chewier. Cut into strips 1 1/2-inch long x 1/2-inch thick. Dip in melted butter, bread by rolling in cheese and crumb mix and fry in hot butter until golden brown. Drain on paper towels. Serve immediately plain or with hot cocktail sauce. *Keep cooking and eat what you want. There will not be any left when you quit cooking, so go outside to enjoy the sunset!*

CRAB MUFFINS

Preparation Time: 10 minutes   *Chef: Jean Thayer*
Chilling Time: freeze   *Yacht: Finesse 60*
Cooking Time: 2-3 minutes
Serves: 6-8

1/4 lb. butter   1/2 tsp. seasoned salt
1 (8 oz.) jar cheese spread,   (Crazy Janes)
   (Kraft Old English)   1/2 tsp. garlic salt
1-1/2 tsp. mayonnaise   1 (7 oz.) can crabmeat
6 English muffins, split

Blend first six ingredients. Spread on muffin halves. Place muffin halves on cookie sheet and freeze. Place in plastic bags in freezer until ready to use. Remove from freezer and cut half into quarters. Broil until browned and heated through. *Serve at once.*

CRAB ROUNDS

Preparation Time: 15 minutes
Cooking Time: 10-12 minutes
Serves: 8

Chef: Barbara Lowe
Yacht: Tri My Way

1 (7 1/2 oz.) can crabmeat
1 Tblsp. green onion, diced
1 cup Swiss cheese, grated
1/2 cup mayonnaise
1 tsp. lemon juice

1/4 tsp. curry powder
1 (10 oz.) package flaky
   refrigerator rolls
1 (5 oz.) can water
   chestnuts, sliced and
   drained

Preheat oven 400 degrees Fahrenheit. Combine crab, green onion, Swiss cheese, mayonnaise, lemon juice, and curry powder. Mix well. Separate each roll into three layers. Place on ungreased baking sheet and spoon on crab mixture. Top each one with the water chestnuts. Bake at 400 for 10-12 minutes.

Chef Nan Gel on Yacht Tuff garnishes with red pepper slices and parsley.

SMOKED OYSTER ROLL

Preparation Time: 10 minutes
Serves: 4-6

Chef: Norma Trease
Yacht: Caroline

1 (8 oz.) package cream
   cheese,softened
1 (3 3/4 oz.) can whole
   smoked oysters,drained

1 tsp. onion, minced
   (optional)
GARNISH: pimiento, capers,
   paprika, dill

On foil, spread slightly softened cream cheese into a rectangle (approx. 9 x 4). Sprinkle with minced onion, if desired. Place drained oysters in a row down the center of cream cheese. Roll lengthwise using foil and place seam down on serving platter. Remove foil with spatula, if needed. Garnish with pimiento, capers, dashes of paprika, and dill. *Serve with assorted crackers.*

GROUPER FINGERS MARINATED IN BEER WITH CREAMY VEGETABLE SAUCE

Preparation Time: 30 minutes
Cooking Time: 10 minutes
Chilling Time: 1-2 hours

Chef: Anita Riley
Yacht: Bright Star

Grouper fillets, cut finger
   size (or other white
    meat fish)
Beer

Salt and pepper
Oil for frying
Flour
GARNISH: lemon slices

SAUCE:
2 Tblsp. butter
1/2 cup green pepper, chopped
1/4 cup celery, chopped
2 Tblsp. onion, chopped
2 Tblsp. carrot, grated
2 Tblsp. all-purpose flour

1/2 tsp. salt
1 cup milk
1/2 cup plain yogurt
Basil leaves
Tarragon

Marinate grouper or other fish in beer. Dry fish well. Roll in seasoned flour and shake off excess flour. Fry in hot oil to a depth of 1/8th inch. Fry quickly, turning once. Allow approximately 10 minutes cooking time, depending on thickness of fish. Drain well. *Serve with creamy vegetable sauce and lemon slices.* Sauce: Mix all ingredients together. Blend well. Chill.

SALMON LOG

Preparation Time: 15 minutes
Chilling Time: 2 hours
Serves: 4-6

Chef: Barbie Haworth
Yacht: Ann-Marie II

1 (15 1/2 oz.) can red salmon
1 (8 oz.) package cream
   cheese, room temperature
1 Tblsp. lemon juice
1 Tblsp. onion, minced

1/4 tsp. salt
1 tsp. horseradish
3/4 cup pecans, chopped
1 Tblsp. fresh parsley,
   chopped
GARNISH: lemon wedges

Drain and flake salmon removing the skin and bones. Combine all ingredients thoroughly. Chill for several hours. Using waxed paper, shape into a log. Roll in pecans and parsley. Re-chill. *Serve with assorted crackers and lemon wedges.*

SMOKED OYSTER STUFFED CHERRY TOMATOES

Preparation Time: 20 minutes
Serves: 6-8

Chefs: Sylvia and Stanley Dabney
Yacht: Native Sun

24 cherry tomatoes
1/4 cup sour cream
1/4 cup mayonnaise,
  (Hellman's)
1/4 tsp. Worcestershire sauce
1/4 cup chives or green
  onions,finely chopped
GARNISH: lemon twists

1 Tblsp. cream cheese,
  optional, adds firmness
  to mixture
1 Tblsp. lemon juice
1-3 tins (24) smoked oysters
1/4 cup fresh parsley,
  chopped

If tomatoes are large, cut in half. Otherwise, just cut the top off. Scoop insides of tomatoes and freeze to add to sauces at a later time. Mix sour cream, mayonnaise, chives, Worcestershire sauce, lemon juice, and cream cheese. Drain oysters. Halve the oysters, if oysters are large. Stuff one into each tomato.   Spoon 1 tsp. mixture over each and sprinkle with parsley. *Serve on a colorful platter or enamel dish on fresh leafy lettuce with lemon twists for color. Left over stuffing is delicious on crackers.*

SEA SCALLOPS SEVICHE

Preparation Time: 30 minutes
Marinating time: 1 hour
Serves: 4

Chef: Jacklyn Johnson Rabinowitz
Yacht: Endless Summer II

1 cup sea scallops, or firm
  fleshed fish
Juice of 4 limes
2 Tblsp. onion, chopped
1 Tblsp. parsley, chopped

2 Tblsp. green pepper,
  chopped
3 Tblsp. olive oil
Salt and freshly ground black
  pepper, to taste

Cut raw scallops in quarters and cover with lime juice. Marinate 1 hour (or overnight is best) in refrigerator. Drain. Combine with onion, parsely, green pepper. Add olive oil. Mix well. Season with salt and pepper. *Serve with melba toast.*

NOTE: Chef Carol Watkins Manto on Yacht Drumbeat puts the scallops in the centre of a serving platter and surrounds them with slices of red and green pepper and black olives with stick frilled toothpicks in them.

COCONUT FRIED SHRIMP

Preparation Time: 30 minutes
Cooking Time: 15 minutes
Serves: 8

Chef: Lisa Hawkins
Hotel: White Bay Sandcastle

BEER BATTER: 1 cup flour
1 tsp. baking powder
1/2 tsp. white pepper
Dash of salt
1 can beer
2 lbs. medium to large shrimp
Flour for dredging

1 (10 oz.) bag flake
   (shredded) coconut
Oil for frying
SAUCE: 1 medium jar
   orange marmalade
2 tsp. Dijon mustard
GARNISH: watercress

Sift dry ingredients for batter, add beer and let sit. Batter will expand, so add beer as needed, but do not make it too thin. Clean shrimp leaving tails intact. Wash shrimp and pat dry with paper towels. Heat oil in heavy skillet or deep fryer. Dredge each shrimp in flour, dip in batter, and then roll in coconut. Fry until golden brown. Drain on paper towels. While shrimp are hot, mix sauce and spoon over shrimp. Arrange on a tray of watercress. *They are very rich. Shrimp may be prepared ahead of time and put in refrigerator until time to fry them.*

NOTE: Serve on sheels as a first course with Filet Marsala, Stuffed Potatoes, and Asparagus In Lemon Butter — recipes in SHIP TO SHORE II.

FLAMBE SHRIMP

Preparation Time: 10 minutes
Cooking Time: 5 minutes
Serves: 6-8

Chef: Jan Robinson
Yacht: Vanity

1/2 lb. bacon, diced
1 lb. shrimp, peeled, cooked,
   and sliced or 2 (7 oz.) cans
12 green olives, sliced thin

1/4 cup golden rum
8 slices pumpernickel bread
Cream cheese

Cook bacon until crunchy. Pour off fat. Spread pumpernickel bread with cream cheese and cut into squares. Place bacon, shrimp, and olives in fireproof serving dish. Pour over rum and ignite. Place dish on a large platter and surround with pumpernickel bread.

SEATTLE SALMON QUICHE

Preparation Time: 15 minutes   *Chefs: Sylvia and Stanley Dabney*
Cooking Time: 60 minutes   *Yacht: Native Sun*
Serves: 6-8

3 scallions, include whites,   1 (10 1/2 oz.) can
   chopped   mushroom soup
1/2 cup sour cream   1 Tblsp. flour
1 cup Cheddar cheese, grated   1 egg
1 unbaked pie shell   2 Tblsp. butter
1 (1 lb.) can salmon, (pick   2 tsp. dill weed
   over spine and bones,   Salt and pepper
   skin removed)

Preheat oven to 325 degrees Fahrenheit. Saute scallions in butter, cool in pan, then add sour cream. Sprinkle 1/2 cup grated Cheddar cheese in bottom of pie shell. Mix salmon, soup, onion and sour cream mixture, flour, egg, butter, and seasonings in a bowl. Then pour over grated cheese in pie shell. Add remaining 1/2 cup cheese on top to cover. Bake 325 degrees for 60 minutes or until "set" in middle. Wait 15 minutes. Cut into squares or small wedges. *Serve cold for hors d'oeuvres with stuffed cherry tomatoes.*

NOTE: Delicious with green salad and garlic bread for dinner. Serve cold with salad and fruit for lunch. Serve "hot" for breakfast with lots of fresh fruit.

PICKLED SHRIMP

Preparation Time: 15 minutes   *Chef: Carole Watkins Manto*
Cooking Time: 10 minutes   *Yacht: Drumbeat*
Marinating Time: overnight
Serves: 8

2 1/2 lbs. shrimp, peeled,   1/4 tsp. celery salt
   deveined and cooked   1/4 tsp. tumerick
1 Tblsp. picklespice   1/2 cup white vinegar
1 Tblsp. Dijon mustard   1 cup oil
1 tsp. horseradish   GARNISH: dill sprigs
1/2 tsp. salt

Peel, devein, and cook shrimp. Combine marinade ingredients (except oil) and bring to a boil. Whip in oil. Pour over cooked shrimp in stainless steel bowl. Marinate overnight or up to 3 days. Arrange on a platter with a sprig of dill on each shrimp. *Serve with Carr's water crackers.*

SHRIMP CHEESE BALL

Preparation Time: 10 minutes   *Chef: Irene McClain*
Chilling Time: 2 hours   *Yacht: Solskin II*
Serves: 8

6 oz. cream cheese
1/2-1 tsp. mustard
1-2 tsp. Worcestershire sauce
1 tsp. lemon juice
1 Tblsp. onion, finely minced

Dash of cayenne pepper
1(4 1/2 oz.) can shrimp,
    broken, well-drained
1/2 cup chopped nuts or
    dried parsley

Mix cream cheese, mustard, Worcestershire sauce, lemon juice, onion, and pepper. Mix in shrimp. Cool for 2 hours or more. Shape into a ball and roll in chopped nuts or parsley. *Serve on a board with crackers and a small bunch of grapes. If no time for cooling, serve as a dip!*

SHRIMP IN SHERRY

Preparation Time: 10 minutes   *Chef: Wendy Smith*
Cooking Time: 5 minutes   *Yacht: Hiya*
Serves: 6

2 oz. butter
1 clove garlic, crushed
1 small onion, finely
    chopped
Salt and pepper

1/4 pint medium dry sherry
1/2 pint cream
1-1/2 lbs. shelled, cooked
    shrimp
GARNISH: chopped parsley

Melt the butter, add the garlic and onion. Fry until softened. Season. Pour in the sherry. Bring to a boil until most of the liquid has evaporated. Add the cream. Simmer till thickened. Check the seasoning, add the shrimp. Pile the mixture into a serving dish. Sprinkle with parsley. *Serve immediately.*

SHRIMP STUFFED CELERY

Preparation Time: 10 minutes
Serves: 6

Chef: Jane Dixon
Yacht: Verano Sin Final

1(4 1/2 oz.) can washed and
   drained broken shrimp
1 tsp. dried chives
3 Tblsp. onion, finely
   chopped
5 black olives, pitted, finely
   chopped

2 Tblsp. slivered almonds
Dash of lemon juice
Enough mayonnaise for
   consistency
Celery stalks, cut in 3"
   pieces

Mix all ingredients thoroughly. Stuff celery and arrange on platter. *Good
quickie hors d'oeuvre. Also good when serving several hors d'oeuvres.*

SWEDISH ENCOUNTER

Preparation Time: 15 minutes
Chilling Time: 1 hour
Serves: 8

Chef: Barbara Stride
Yacht: All Is Best

1 (8oz.) jar pickled herring
   fillets
1 sweet red pepper, chopped
6-8 gherkins, chopped
2 shallots, finely chopped

White wine vinegar
1 cup sour cream
2 Tblsp. green onions,
   chopped
Freshly ground black pepper

Drain herring and slice into bite size pieces. Add red pepper, gherkins,
shallots, and cover with wine vinegar. In a separate bowl, mix sour
cream, onions, and pepper to taste. Chill both at least 1 hour. *Serve with
crackers or triangles of toast.*

LOBSTER SPREAD

Preparation Time: 15 minutes
Cooking Time: 2 minutes
Serves: 4-6

Chef: Jan Stoughton
Yacht: Mirage

1-1 1/2 cups lobster meat,
** shredded**
2 Tblsp. Miracle Whip
1/2 stack of Ritz crackers
** (approx. 15)**
Worcestershire sauce, to taste

Chili or paprika, to taste
Tabasco sauce, to taste
White pepper, to taste
Lime juice, to taste
Party rye bread

Crush crackers, add to lobster. Add Miracle Whip enough so that mixture is moist. Add the rest of ingredients to taste, depending on how spicy or hot you like it. Paprika can be used instead of chili powder to keep it mild. Mix well and spread on slices of bread and broil. Be sure to use Miracle Whip and not mayonnaise!

EASY MARLIN SPREAD

Preparation time: 10 minutes
Serves: 6

Chef: Donna Keller
Yacht: Adela

1/2 lb. smoked marlin
2-3 Tblsp. mayonnaise
1 small onion, diced

Salt and pepper, to taste
GARNISH: carrot, celery,
** green pepper**

Shred marlin in bowl. Mix 2-3 Tblsp. of mayonnaise, onion, salt, and pepper. Spread on a bed of lettuce. Surround with an assortment of crackers

NOTE: I shape mixture into a fish using a carrot for an eye and celery or green pepper for stripes in tail.

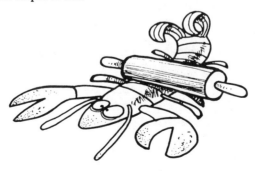

SMOKED MARLIN SPREAD

Preparation Time: 10 minutes   *Chef: Lisa Ferry*
Chilling Time: 1/2 hour   *Yacht: Memories*
Serves: 4-6

1/4 lb. smoked marlin
6 oz. cream cheese
1 small onion, finely chopped
1 stalk celery, finely chopped
2 dashes tabasco

4 dashes Worcestershire sauce
1 Tblsp. horseradish or to
   taste
1 Tblsp. lemon juice
GARNISH: tomato wedges,
   parsley sprigs

Remove any skin from smoked marlin. Break into chunks and combine with cream cheese in food processor til smooth. Transfer to bowl and add remaining ingredients. Serve in small souffle dish garnished with tomato wedges and parsley sprigs. *Accompany with rye crisps, flat bread, or your favorite cracker.*

HOT MUSHROOM SPREAD

Preparation Time: 15 minutes   *Chef: Donna Jaggard*
Cooking Time: 10 minutes   *Yacht: Thorobred*
Serves: 6-8

4 slices bacon
8 oz. mushrooms, chopped
1 clove garlic, minced
1 onion, chopped
2 Tblsp. flour
1/4 tsp. salt

1/8 tsp. pepper
1 (8 oz.) package cream
   cheese, cubed
1 tsp. soy sauce
1/2 cup sour cream
2 tsp. Worcestershire sauce

Cook bacon; set aside. Reserve 2 Tblsp. drippings. Saute mushrooms, garlic, and onion in drippings until tender and most of the liquid is evaporated.   Stir in flour, salt and pepper.   Add cream cheese, Worcestershire sauce, and soy sauce. Stir until cheese is melted. Stir in sour cream and crumbled bacon. *Serve hot with crackers.*

CAROLE'S OYSTER SPREAD

Preparation Time: 5 minutes   *Chef: Carole Watkins Manto*
Serves: 6   *Yacht: Drumbeat*

1 (8 oz.) package cream   Red currant preserves
  cheese, room temperature   1 box Triscuits or crackers
1 tin (24) smoked oysters,   of your choice
  drained

Using a fork, combine oysters and cream cheese. Mix well. Shape into a small mound. Top with perserves. *Surround with triscuits or crackers of your choice!*

BUTTERY SALMON SPREAD

Preparation Time: 10 minutes   *Chef: Jean Thayer*
Chilling Time: 1 hour   *Yacht: Finesse 60*
Serves: 6

1 (7 oz.) can red salmon,   1/4 tsp. hot pepper sauce
  remove skin and bones   4 Tblsp. butter, melted
1 Tblsp. and 1 tsp. lemon   1/2 cup sour cream
  juice   GARNISH: minced chives
1/2 tsp. Dijon mustard

In a blender or food processor, puree salmon, lemon juice, mustard, and hot sauce. Pour in butter and puree. Scrape salmon mix into a small bowl and stir in the sour cream. Refrigerate, covered for one hour or more. Sprinkle with chives before serving. *Serve with crackers, French bread, or raw vegetables (for dipping).*

ENDIVE DIPPERS

Preparation Time: 15 minutes   *Chef: Betsi Dwyer*
Serves: 6   *Yacht: September Morn*

2-3 heads Endive or Romaine   Alfalfa sprouts, chives, or
1 package soft herb cheese,   fresh parsley
  Garlic or Boursin

Remove ends of endive and discard outer leaves. Rinse and dry leaves. Place a tsp. of cheese on the square end of each leaf and top with a few sprouts of chopped fresh parsley or chives. Arrange in a circle on serving platter with extra cheese in the center, if you like. *Use endive leaves instead of crackers or chips for a low calorie snack with any dip.*

ARTICHOKE BITES

Preparation Time: 20 minutes   *Chef: Jean Crook*
Cooking Time: 30-35 minutes   *Yacht: Dileas*
Makes: 25 squares

2 (6 oz.) jars artichoke   1/2 tsp. salt
   heatrs, marinated   1/4 tsp. dried oregano
1 onion, finely chopped   Hot pepper sauce, to taste
1 large clove garlic, minced   Black pepper, freshly ground
4 eggs, beaten   2 cups Cheddar cheese,
1/4 cup fine, dry breadcrumbs   shredded

Preheat oven to 325 degrees Fahrenheit. Drain artichokes reserving 1/4 cup of marinade. Chop artichokes into 1/2-inch pieces. In skillet, heat reserved marinade. Cook onion and garlic until softened about 5 minutes. In bowl, beat eggs, stir in onion, garlic mix, bread crumbs, salt, oregano, and hot pepper sauce and pepper, to taste. Stir in cheese, then artichokes. Spoon into buttered 8-inch square baking dish. Bake at 325 for 30-35 minutes or until set. Let cool for a few minutes. Cut into squares. *Serve warm or cold.*

CAPONATA

Preparation Time: 10 minutes   *Chef: Carol Lowe*
Cooking Time: 45 minutes   *Yacht: Natasha*
Serves: 8

1/4 cup olive oil   1 (6 oz.) can tomato paste
1/2 green pepper, diced   1 tsp. sugar
1 medium onion, diced   1 tsp. salt
1 medium eggplant, peeled,   1 Tblsp. white vinegar
   cubed   1 tsp. oregano
1 garlic clove, crushed   1/4 cup water
1/2 lb. mushrooms, sliced

Saute green pepper and onion in oil.   Add eggplant, garlic, and mushrooms. Simmer 10 minutes. Add all other ingredients and simmer 30 minutes. Can refrigerate up to 1 week. *Serve with toasted pita bread.*

PACKED CELERY STICKS

Preparation Time: 20 minutes   *Chef: Jeanne Felton*
Serves: 6-8   *Yacht: Prego*

6 long stalks washed celery
  with ends trimmed
  diagonally
1 (8 oz.) package cream
  cheese, room temperature
8 oz. salami, 3-inch
  diameter, thinly sliced

SAUCE: 1/2 cup brown
  mustard (Grey Poupon)
Dash of garlic powder
1/4 cup mayonnaise
2 tsp. lime juice
Colored or fancy cocktail
  toothpicks

Cut celery into 3-4 inch pieces with diagonal or crinkle cut. Spread cream cheese in hollow of celery sticks. Wrap each with salami or similar meat and secure with toothpicks. Combine remaining ingredients and serve as a dip. *Arrange on platter or plate with dip in small bowl in center, with sticks radiating from it like spokes of a wheel or do an off center arrangement.*

GREEN CHILE WONTONS AND TOMATO CORIANDER SAUCE

Preparation Time: 20 minutes   *Chef: Barbara Lowe*
Cooking Time: 20 minutes   *Yacht: Tri My Way*
Serves: 8

SAUCE: 1 (7 1/2 oz.) can
  tomatoes, undrained
2 Tblsp. fresh parsley
1 small green onion
1 Tblsp. butter
2 cloves garlic
1/4 tsp. paprika

1/2 lb. Monterey Jack
  cheese, grated
1 (14 oz.) can green chilies,
  chopped
1 package wonton skins
Oil for frying

Combine sauce ingredients in food processor or bowl. Blend until finely chopped. Transfer to sauce pan and bring to a boil. Reduce heat and simmer for 5 minutes. Serve warm.

Mix grated cheese and chopped green chilies together. Put one tablespoon on each wonton skin and wrap according to package directions. Fry in hot oil.

BAKED HEARTS OF PALM

Preparation Time: 15 minutes   *Chef: Kimberly Foote*
Cooking Time: 10 minutes   *Yacht: Oklahoma Crude II*
Serves: 6

1 (14 oz.) can hearts of palm, drained
Parsley
Paprika

Dark green lettuce leaves
1 egg, beaten
1/4 cup butter, melted
1/2 cup bread crumbs, (Progresso)

Preheat oven to 400 degrees Fahrenheit. Drain hearts of palm. Slice large pieces in halves or thirds lengthwise. Dip each piece in beaten egg, then in bread crumbs. Place in a small baking pan and pour melted butter over them. Bake 10 minutes at 400. To serve: place a layer of dark lettuce on a plate. Arrange hearts of palm. Sprinkle with paprika and parsley.

MEXICAN MEDLEY

Preparation Time: 15 minutes   *Chef: Cindy Harhen*
Serves: 6   *Yacht: Impervious Cover*

1 (16 oz.) can refried beans
1 package taco seasoning mix
1 large avocado, peeled, destoned, mashed mixed with 1 cup sour cream
3 medium tomatoes, chopped

1 (4 oz.) can green chilies, chopped
Black olives, sliced
1 bag tortilla chips
1 cup Cheddar cheese, grated

In a glass bowl, arrange the above ingredients ending with the black olives on top. Place in the center of a large round tray surrounded with tortilla chips.

NOTE: This fun hors d'oeuvre is a real "wow-er" with very little work on the chef's part! I usually put a serving knife nearby to help guests eat every drop and they will!

MUSHROOMS
STUFFED WITH MOUSSE TRUFFLES

Preparation Time: 20-30 minutes   *Chef: Diana Horn*
Cooking Time: 10 minutes   *Yacht: Rangga*

2-3 large mushrooms,   **Flour**
   per person   **Egg**
1/4-1/2 lb. mousse truffles   **Seasoned breadcrumbs**
Oil for frying

Remove stems and clean mushrooms. Pat dry. Fill mushrooms with mousse truffles. Roll in flour, dip in egg and breadcrumbs. Quickly fry in hot oil till golden brown - turning once. *Serve with large napkins. They tend to squirt juices when bitten into!*

STUFFED MUSHROOMS

Preparation Time: 20 minutes   *Chef: Emily Welch*
Cooking Time: 15 minutes   *Yacht: Siren's Song*
Serves: 6

18 large mushrooms   **Dash tabasco**
1 (10 oz.) package frozen   **2 Tblsp. butter**
   spinach   **1/4 cup Parmesan cheese,**
1/4 cup breadcrumbs, (Italian)   **grated**
1/2 tsp. garlic, minced   **GARNISH:cherry tomatoes,**
1 tsp. parsley   **cheese cubes, or sprigs**
1 tsp. oregano   **of parsley**

Preheat oven to 350 degrees Fahrenheit. Wash wipe dry, and remove stems from mushrooms. Place on cookie sheet. Cook spinach with a small amount of water just until thawed. Drain and add remaining ingredients except 2 Tblsp. Parmesan cheese. Mix well and stuff mushrooms. Sprinkle rest of Parmesan over each mushroom. Bake for 15 minutes. *Serve on tray with cherry tomatoes and cheese cubes or alone with sprigs of parsley.*

NOTE: Good accompaniment to New York strip steaks, Caesar salad and baked potatoes.

PICKLED ONIONS AND CHEESE

Preparation Time: 5 minutes   *Chef: Jan Robinson*
Serves: 4-6   *Yacht: Vanity*

1 (14 oz.) jar pickled   **1 lb. sharp Cheddar cheese**
English onions

Cut onions in half, if large. Cut Cheddar cheese in cubes. Stick a frilly toothpick through the onion and then the cheese. Serve on a decorative tray.

Question: Do you know why the onion fell off the table?
Answer: Because it was pickled.

Note: Canned pineapple chunks with cheddar cheese is also good.

SPINACH SPANAKOPITES

Preparation Time: 10 minutes   *Chef: CJ Burns*
Cooking Time: 20 minutes   *Yacht: Grace*
Serves: 6

1 (10 oz.) package frozen   **2 dashes garlic powder**
spinach   **1/4 cup butter, melted**
1 small onion, chopped   **1 sheet puff pastry filo**
1/4 cup Parmesan cheese   **dough**
2 dashes salt and pepper   **4 oz. cream cheese**
1 egg, beaten   **Paprika**

Preheat oven to 375 degrees Fahrenheit. Defrost spinach in a bowl. Use a microwave, if possible. Add egg, onion, Parmesan cheese, salt and pepper, and garlic. Brush the center of trifolded filo dough with the melted butter. Spread with 4 oz. cream cheese and 1/2 of the spinach mixture. Fold over the right side of dough. Brush with butter and spread on remaining spinach mixture. Fold over the section of dough and brush with butter. Sprinkle with paprika. Score at an angle with a sharp knife. Bake at 375 for about 20 minutes. Let cool for 10 minutes before cutting into diamonds.

NOTE: Also excellent served with lamb or veal chops with sherry sauce or prime rib for a main course.

THE BAR STOCK

To satisfy just about anyone's preference, you should stock your bar with a 750 milliliter bottle of each of the following:

* Bourbon
* Brandy, Port, Sherry
* Gin
* Red and White wine
* Rum (Light and Dark)
* Scotch
* Tequilla
* Vermouth (Sweet and Dry)
* Vodka
* Any assortment of Liqueurs

Along with the alcohol, you must have mixers. Here is a good selection from which to choose.

* Canned juices: tomato, pineapple, cranberry
* Club soda or seltzer
* Colas
* Fresh fruit juices: orange, grapefruit, lemon, lime
* Ginger ale
* Lemon/Lime sodas
* Sugar syrup
* Tonic or quinine water
* Water

Specialty and tropical drinks require special additions to your bar stock. Here is a good listing.

* Coconut milk
* Cream (Light, Heavy, and Whipping)
* Fruits of a tropical nature
* Grenadine syrup
* Orgeat syrup
* Papaya juice
* Passion fruit juice
* Raspberry syrup
* Triple sec

Garnishes make the drinks very pleasing to the eye. They are a great addition to your bar. Add these:

* Bananas
* Bitters
* Cassis (Black Currant Syrup)
* Celery Sticks
* Cinnamon sticks
* Cocktail onions
* Cucumber
* Horseradish
* Lemons
* Limes
* Maraschino cherries
* Mint leaves
* Oranges
* Pineapple
* Strawberries
* Stuffed olives
* Tabasco sauce
* Worcestershire sauce

In addition to the above bar supplies, it is also good to have:

* Salt
* Sugar (Granulated and Powdered)
* Pepper

EQUIPMENT

Having the right equipment on hand in your bar whether you are on land or sea makes the job easier. The following tools are essential:

1. Can and bottle openers
2. Corkscrew
3. Traditional corkscrew
4. Long spoon or glass stirring rod
5. Coil-rimmed bar strainer
6. A shaker or mixing glass
7. Paring knife for garnishes
8. Wooden muddler for mashing fruits, etc.
9. Large glass pitcher
10. Fruit juicer
11. Measuring spoons
12. A jigger glass
13. Ice bucket and tongs
    Electric blender
    Glassware
    Fancy stir sticks or decorations
    Napkins

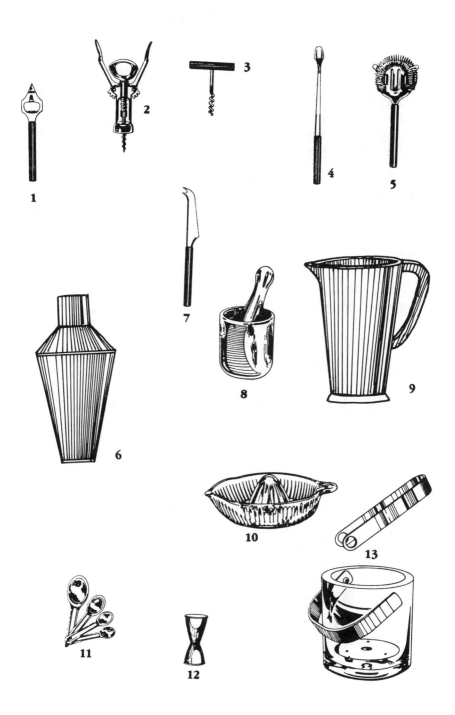

GLASSWARE

The glass in which you serve a drink is more than just a medium for transferring liquor from bottle to drinker. It frames the contents for the eye, directs the aroma to the nose, and touches the lips before the liquid releases its flavor. It is important to use attractive glassware to make drinking all the more pleasureable.

There are a fascinating variety of glasses available. Here are illustrations of the basic glasses that we feel would best suit the drink to be prepared. Each cocktail recipe has a drawing of one of these shapes beside it along with the name of each glass:

Goblet	Old Fashioned
Champagne Flute	Fancy
Liqueur Pousse - cafe	Cocktail
Tulip	Glass Mug
Lager	Whiskey Tumbler
Collins	Balloon
Highball	Brandy Snifter
Champagne Saucer	

GLASS PREPARATION

There are three basic ways to prepare glasses beforehand: chilling, frosting, and sugar frosting.

CHILLING GLASSES: Always chill before you fill. There are three ways:

1. Put glasses in the refrigerator or freeze a couple of hours before using them.
2. Fill the glasses with cracked ice and stir the ice before pouring in the drink.
3. Bury the glasses in cracked ice just before using.

FROSTING GLASSES: For a large lasting frost, dip the glasses in water and while still dipping, place them in your freezer for 2 or 3 hours.

SUGAR FROSTING GLASSES: Moisten the rim of a prechilled glass with a slice of lime or lemon and then dip the rim into sugar or powdered sugar. For margaritas, rub the rim of the glass with a lime, invert glass and dip in course salt.

TO STIR OR NOT TO STIR

To mix a pitcher of cocktails properly, you need to stir for at least 10 seconds. If carbonated mixers are added, you only need to stir a couple of times.

WHEN TO SHAKE

Shake the shaker, not yourself, or use an electric blender for any drink made with juices, sugar, egg, or cream. Strain cocktails into a glass through a coil rim strainer.

POURING

Drinks wilt. Pour them as soon as you make them. Leftovers should be discarded from the shaker or it will become a watery grave by the time you are ready to make "seconds".

USING FRUIT AND FRUIT JUICES

Always try to use fresh fruit when you are making drinks. Wash the outside peel before using. Lemons, limes, or oranges should be rolled back and forth with the palm of the hand on a cutting board before they are cut for squeezing. (You can also microwave a few seconds.) This softens the flesh and you can get more juice.

When recipes call for a twist of lemon peel, it should be cut just before serving to preserve the oils. Rub a strip of peel around the rim of the glass to deposit the oil on it. Then twist the peel so that the oil will drop into the drink. Then drop in the peel.

SIMPLE SYRUP OR SUGAR SYRUP

Simple syrup is often easier to use to sweeten drinks than sugar as it blends without prolonged shaking or stirring. The recipe follows:

SIMPLE SYRUP: Bring 1 cup of water to boil and stir in 1 cup of sugar. Simmer a couple of minutes until sugar has dissolved. Cool. Makes approximately 1 cup.

Use fresh fruit !

BAR MEASUREMENTS

Dash (or splash)
Less than 1/8 teaspoon

1 teaspoon (bar spoon)
60 drops or 1/3 tablespoon

1 Tablespoon
3 teaspoons or 3/8 ounces

2 Tablespoons
1 fluid ounce

1 pony
1 ounce

1 jigger (bar measuring glass)
1 1/2 ounce

4 Tablespoons
1/4 cup

5 1/3 Tablespoons
1/3 cup

6 Tablespoons
3/8 cup

8 Tablespoons
1/2 cup

10 2/3 Tablespoons
2/3 cup

12 Tablespoons
3/4 cup

1 wine glass
8 ounces

16 Tablespoons
1 cup or 8 ounces

1 cup
1/2 pint or 8 fluid ounces

2 cups
1 pint

1 pint
16 ounces

1 quart
2 pints

2.1 pints
1.05 quarts or .26 gallons

2 quarts
1/2 gallon

4 quarts
1 gallon

AHOY MATES!

TOASTS FROM AROUND THE WORLD

American	Bottoms Up
Arabian	Be Sihetak
Austrian	Prosit
Bohemian	Naz Dar
Brazilian	Saude
Chinese	Nien Nien Ju E
Czechoslovakian	Na Zdravie
Danish	Skaal
Dutch	Proost
Egyptian	Fee Sihetak
English	Cheers
Estonian	Tervist
Finnish	Kippis
French	A Votre Sante
German	Prosit
Greek	Eis Igian
Hebrew	L'chayim
Hungarian	Kedves Egeszsegere
Irish	Salinte
Italian	A la Salute
Japanese	Kampai
New Zealand	Down the Hatch
Norwegian	Skal
Russian	Na Zdorovia
Scottish	Shlante
Spanish	Salud
Swedish	Skol
Thai	Sawasdi
Welsh	Iechyd Da
Yugoslavian	Na Zdravie

PARTICIPATING YACHTS

<u>Adela</u>: *Captain Jerry Keller, Chef Donna Keller*

Adela is a 50' sailing yacht comfortably equipped for a cruising vacation you'll never forget.   Come sail clear waters, walk on white sandy beaches and enjoy enchanting tropical nights.   Donna and Jerry look forward to making you their friends.

<u>All Is Best</u>: *Captain Chuck Bentley, Chefs Barbara Stride and Ruth Gardner*

This elegant 70' Camper and Nicholson Ketch will accommodate up to six guests in three private staterooms.   The yacht comes complete with air conditioning, stereo, television, VHS system, plenty of hot water,   and an icemaker.   Beyond sailing you can experience windsurfing, water-skiing, snorkeling, and fishing.   Make your plans early and we'll meet you anywhere in the Caribbean.

<u>Almost Heaven</u>: *Captain Mark Rabinowitz, Chef Jacklyn Johnson Rabinowitz*

A limited edition 51' Morgan Ketch, beautifully appointed with a customized teak interior, she takes four guests in two double staterooms. Equipped with air conditioner, stereo, VHS, video camera, windsurfer, and snorkeling gear.   Jackie excells in fine meal presentations, and Captain Mark is an entertaining raconteur.   Come join us ... it's Almost Heaven! NOTE: Captain Mark Rabinowitz and Chef Jacklyn Johnson Rabinowitz are on Yacht Endless Summer II as of June 1986.

<u>Ann Marie II</u>: *Captain Ken Haworth, Chef Barbie Haworth*

Ann Marie II, a 37' steel Zealand Yawl was built in Holland 30 years ago.   This classic sailboat is unsurpassed in beauty inside and out.   Ken and Barbie Haworth take two guests only, per charter, offering a sailing vacation you'll always cherish.

<u>Antipodes</u>: *Captains Manfred and Dieter Zerbe, Chef Kim Turk*

Ocean 60' Schooner.   Can accommodate up to 8 guests in her 4 identical staterooms.   Her captains have both chartered successully since 1973.   They have the valuable expertise necessary for a successul trip.   Let Antipodes float your way on a Caribbean vacation unlike any you have ever experienced.

<u>Bright Star</u>: *Captain Edwin E. Riley, Chef Anita Riley*

Come sail this beautiful yacht that comes from The Moorings fleet.

Calypso: *Captain and Chef Pat Rowley*
Enjoy the islands aboard Calypso, a 1982 Morgan 51'. Whether it be swimming and snorkeling in a secluded cove, or sunning on her spacious decks, Calypso offers everything you might want for a memorable vacation. Calypso is available for charter in the Caribbean, November through May, and New England during the summer months.

Caroline: *Captain Ann Avery, Chef Norma Trease*
55' Camper-Nicholson, 2-4 guests.

Champagne: *Captain Peo Stenberg, Chefs Peo and Marilyn Stenberg*
Peo and Marilyn combine all their years of catering and sailing experience to make your charter vacation truly memorable. Champagne has luxurious accommodations for 4 guests, in 2 double cabins, with all the comforts you need and deserve. Come sail with us and discover the secret spots in Paradise.

Chaparral: *Captains Daniel and Shannon Webster, Chef Shannon Webster*
Chaparral is a Gulfstar 60', boasting excellent accommodations and a wide variety of culinary delights. She is operated and maintained by Captains Dan and Shannon Webster. Their skill and knowledge of the islands is extensive, but their hospitality is what all guests remember best.

Chinook I: *Captain Ron Neilson, Chef Anne Mallon*
"Chinook I" is an Olympic 47' for Mediterranean chartering. Anne and Ron work together on deck and in the galley to insure that you enjoy memorable days feasting on the food, wine, winds, and waters. Dine below in the spacious, elegant saloon or on deck under the sun or stars. Welcome aboard!

Cinderella: *Captain and Chef Jim Carroza*
Cinderella is a captain only charter. Guests are encouraged to participate in sailing, navigation, and cooking. Family cruises and children are welcome.

Concrescent: *Captain and Chef Sandye Bullard*

Drumbeat: *Captain Richard Manto, Chef Carole Watkins Manto*
Drumbeat is an Irwin 65' designed just for charter. Four double cabins with their own heads and showers. Luxurious and spacious. Lots of toys, lots of attention, and lots of gourmet food!! "Drumbeat" - The Ultimate Caribbean Vacation!

Dileas: *Captain David Crook, Chef Jean Crook*
Dileas is a 42' out island Morgan. Jean and Dave are owner-operators and have been sailing in the Virgins for 15 years and chartering for 6 years. They enjoy being with people of all walks of life.

Emerald Lady: *Captain Paul Array, Chef Mardy Array*
The world is yours aboard ... the Emerald Lady! Join Paul and Mardy aboard the newly constructed fiberglas world cruising Ketch, and let them introduce you to their exciting world of ocean cruising adventures. Emerald Lady has the ambience of an old world galleon with every modern convenience. Your wants ... your desires ... your fantasies ... are all aboard the Lady!

Emerald Lady: *Captain and Chef Richard George*
Aboard Emerald Lady, a 65' Irwin, we will take you to secluded coves, beautiful beaches, and interesting and exciting sites ashore. For the finest food and sailing, join us on Emerald Lady.

Endless Summer II: *Captain Barry Rice, Chef Rosalind Rice*
Recipe for the Ultimate Caribbean Experience:
Ingredients: 3 Friendly British Crew
                Up to 8 Congenial Guests
                4 Double Bedded Staterooms, Bathroom en suite
Method: Set temperature at desired sunshine level. Blend ingredients together in a 65' sailing vessel. Add a touch of luxury and wine to taste. Brown slowly for at least one week. NOTE: As of June 1986, Captain Mark Rabonowitz and Chef Jacklyn Johnson Rabinowitz are on Endless Summer II. (Formerly on Almost Heaven.)

Excalibur: *Captain Willie McCormick, Chef Charlotte Robinson*
Excalibur is truly a world class cruising yacht. Her sensible design gives her excellent sailing performance coupled with impeccible appointments below. Enjoy sumptuous cuisine surrounded by teak, oak, and polished bronze. Pampered by Excalibur's crew, caressed by tropical sun and breezes, this will certainly be a memorable vacation.

Falcon Gentle: *Captain David Reil, Chef Wendy Mitchell*
Falcon Gentle is a Landfall 43' designed for the charter trade out of Newport in the summer and USVI in the winter. Taking a capacity of 4 enables you personalized service, food, and travel that you'll be talking about for months to come.

Fancy Free: *Captain Tom Miller, Chef Casey Miller*
Fancy Free is a 51' comfortable Cutter. Two private double cabins for 4 guests with separate crew quarters. Fully equipped for windsurfing, snorkeling, and enthusiastic sailing. Dine on classic cuisine customized to your taste. Join us for the total vacation experience.

Fantasy: *Captain Fred Stetson, Chef D. Stetson*
Fantasy, a Gulfstar 43' Ketch, is a fast, comfortable and beautifully appointed sailing yacht. She offers 2-4 guests the maximum of comfort often found on larger vessels. Dine on international cuisine, the very best from around the world. You'll never forget the Virgin Islands after you experience the Fantasy.

Finesse 60: *Captain Doug Thayer, Chef Jean Thayer*

finesse (fi'-nesse) n. Gulfstar 60'. 1. Cruising a. relating to sailors-take wheel, set course. b. For non-sailors-a moveable resort (refer to beaches, dining) 2. Beaches of or pertaining to quiet coves, snorkeling, windsurfing. 3. Dining-fine food and drink. 4. Accommodations for two, four, or six. 5. Families-see Welcome. YACHT FINESSE defines it all!

Flute: *Captain Rik Van Rensselaer, Chef Lee Ann La Casa*

Flute is special in every way for a couple, two couples, or a family of six. Happy, fun, relaxing, congenial, and the food is fabulous! Come sail on Flute, and let us take you "away from it all" into paradise on the ultimate sailing holiday.

Flying Ginny V: *Captain Sey Owens, Chef Carol Owens*

Flying Ginny V is a Morgan 60' Schooner, one of The Moorings fleet of crewed yachts - marked by captains with impeccible sailing credentials and cooks with gourmet culinary skills. Sail with us and share warm memories of Paradise.

Freight Train: *Captain George Banker, Chef Candice Carson*

A boat who sails as fast as her name
Operated by owners in the charter game
Escape the cold, the frazzles, and the mundane
Let your body grow healthy, your mind grow sane
If you have gotten this far, you know poets we're not
But good cooks and fun people reside on this yacht.

Grace: *Captain George Yerkes, Chef C.J. Burns*

Grace is a 50' Cutter owned by its captain specializing in romantic cruises in the BVI, VI, or Down Island. With a divemaster, George is sure to fill your platter with fresh fish, lobster, and champagne. 2 guests to a maximum of 4.

Graciet: *Captain Tom Gavin, Chef Jane Glancy*

Graciet combines a noteworthy racing heritage graced with complete luxury appointments, a unique combination. There are three double guests staterooms with heads and separate crew quarters. There is a huge saloon that takes advantage of her 15 foot beam and the entire yacht is air conditioned.

Helios: *Captain Michael Minett, Chef Dawn Drell*

On Helios, having fun is important to us! Along with great cuisine and warm hospitality, enjoy learning to windsurf (we have 2), swimming, snorkeling, or relaxing in the hammock. Come sailing on this beautiful and graceful swan and discover what Paradise is really all about!

Hiya: *Captian Andy Smith, Chef Wendy Smith*

When next summers gone and you want some sun, join us on this 59' Swan.

Impervious Cover: *Captain Paul Soule, Chef Cindy Harhen*

Impervious Cover is a Gulfstar 62' (Hull #1). The first of her kind in the chartering fleet. Captain Paul Soule and Chef/Mate Cindy Harhen are avid sailors and water sports enthusiasts. Both enjoy cooking. Paul comes from the seafood-rich eastern shore of Delaware and specializes in seafood. Cindy enjoys traditional as well as exotic cuisine.

Jolie Brise: *Captain Mike Burrill, Chef Geli Burrill*

Not all the brokers can be wrong! Jolie Brise, winner of prize for boat which brokers would themselves most like to charter in 1984-85 boat show in the Virgin Islands. This very special and exciting 62' C+C Ketch only takes four guests in comfortable elegant decadence.

Memories: *Captain Scott Palmer, Chef Lisa Ferry*

Memories - a Nelson Merrick designed Morgan 45' Sloop custom-fitted with every possible amenity for sailing and recreation. The large forward cabin with shower and head ensuite and complete crew quarters aft provide total privacy to our one couple (and honeymoon!) charters.

Mistral: *Captain Russ Fielden, Chef Laura Greces*

Come sail Mistral, a 50' Sloop that really sails! She was built in 1983 by Morgan, especially for Caribbean chartering. Russ and Laura really love these islands and delight in taking you "off the beaten track". We'll be happy to help you sharpen your sailing skills or let you relax.

Mirage: *Captain Nigel Helps, Chefs Jan Stoughton and Cathy Heidenreich*

Mirage, an Island of Luxury! Be pampered in the style to which you would love to become accustomed. Live the life of luxury aboard the 140' World Class Motor Yacht.

Natasha: *Captain Peter Morris, Chefs Georgina Morris and Carol Lowe*

Natasha is an 83' Camper and Nicholson Ketch designed by Jon Bannenburg. She sleeps 6 in three air conditioned cabins, two with double berths. Natasha has a crew of four and provides gourmet dining, water-skiing, windsurfing, diving, and snorkeling. Come join us!

Native Sun: *Captains and Chefs Stanley and Sylvia Dabney*

Valiant 40' (Hull #9). Specializing in day charters, snorkeling, lunch, and entertaining stories of 40,000 miles offshore sailing and ten years of living aboard Native Sun. We welcome every guest as a friend and treat each new friend as family. We consider beautiful Honeymoon Bay on Water Island, our home in the islands, the place where our love affair with sailing began 16 years ago.

Ocean Carnival: *Captains Bob and Didgie Belschmer, Chef Didgie Belschmer*

This Ocean 60' Schooner is a full boat to sail. She has three equal cabins containing a double and single bunk in each. The menu is sumptuous and enjoy our tropical drink of the day!

Oklahoma Crude II: *Captain Colin Rees, Chef Kimberly Foote*
This Irwin 52's luxurious accommodations make living aboard a pleasure. The interior of this Ketch is custom designed for charter. The galley is fully stocked with crystal and silver for serving Caribbean delicacies. An experienced crew promises to take you into the most relaxing, enjoyable holiday possible.

Once Upon A Time: *Captain Harry Newton, Chef Nicky Cahi*
Once Upon A Time, there was a beautiful 41' Catamaran built in England for chartering in the Caribbean. News of her luxury, elegance and comfort spread far and wide and soon people arrived to discover the continuing story of this lovely yacht.

Passages: *Captain Howard Erickson, Chef Ada Bols*
Passages is a 53' ketch chartering out of Oceanside New York. Can accommodate up to six guest. Fine foods, wines, hors d'oeuvre are yours to enjoy aboard Passages. Fabulous fun for everyone!

Prego: *Captain Gary Felton , Chef Jeanne Felton*
Prego is a 60' Gulfstar , center cockpit, double-headsail Sloop. In bristol condition, Prego boasts three separate double staterooms including a private head for each. Ask for Captian Felton at The Moorings to receve your gourmet delights, sailing pleasures and best vacation.

Promenade: *Captain David Dugdale, Chef Fiona Baldrey*
Magnificent 60' Trimaran taking up to 10 guest: "Fantastic trip, thoroughly enjoyed all the water activities especially the scuba diving. Great food and wonderful service." A quote from our guest book.

Raby Vaucluse: *Captain Bill Gibson, Chef Liz Thomas*
This Morgan 46' is built for charter. She is very comfortable below with two guest staterooms and private heads. Bill Gibson is highly competent and experienced. Liz Thomas takes great pride in her meals prepared aboard. Let Raby Vaucluse and her crew make this your most enjoyable vacation.

Rangga: *Captain Rod Novak, Chefs Diana Horn and Edward Tuleja*
Seventy-three feet of fun with spacious teak decks over 5 doubles and 3 heads. This cruising Schooner combines the best of all worlds. Superb sailing with luxury accommodations. International cuisine, professional mixology, live and recorded music, dancing in the moonlight, and even some skiing, snorkeling, diving, or windsurfing. Power lounging instructions available.

Royono: *Captain Ben Sheets, Chef Sarah Sheets*

Sailing aboard Royono, an 85' Alden/Herreshoff Yawl, is to experience the aura of a time past when life was more leisurely, and yachts were designed by the old masters with an eye towards elegance and beauty. Ben and Sarah Sheets welcome guests aboard for exceptional sailing, excellent food, and gracious service and company.

Ruach: *Captain Michael Vegiard, Chef Judith Meyers Vegiard*

September Morn: *Captain Eric Unterborn, Chef Betsi Dwyer*

Siren's Song: *Captain Sam Welch, Chef Emily Welch*

Welcome aboard this 52' Irwin for a holiday of a lifetime.

Solskin II: *Captain John Long, Chef Irene McClain*

Solskin II is a 37' Alberg Yawl where pleasure is the name of the game for our day sailing guests.

S.S. Paj: *Captain Michael Szarowicz, Chef Karen Williams*

S.S. Paj is a 46' Catamaran that offers a feast for all the senses. Beautifully decorated with 3 spacious double cabins, a large airy saloon, and a huge covered cockpit for open air dining. The cuisine is sensational and Michael and Karen will be your fun loving hosts.

Stowaway: *Captain Alan Balfour, Chef Chris Balfour*

Thorobred: *Captain George B. Brown, Chef Donna Jaggard*

Thorobred, an owner-operated semi-custom Morgan 41', has been chartering in the Caribbean since 1979. George and Donna will make your chartering vacation a most memorable one.

Tri My Way: *Captains Warwick and Barbara Lowe, Chef Barbara Lowe*

Tri My Way is a contemporary, spacious new Trimaran, capable of accommodating up to 10 guests. She will provide total luxury and privacy for 6. With activities that range from scuba diving to windsurfing, she is literally a floating resort. Come sail MY WAY with Captains Warwick and Barbara Lowe for an unforgettable holiday.

Tuff: *Captain Jim Oosterhoudt, Chefs Nan Gee and Margo Muckey*

It is a tough world unless you're sailing in the Virgin Islands on yacht "TUFF". TUFF is a C +C 48', with spacious accommodations for 2 or 4 persons and all the amenities you would expect on a first class yacht. Jim and Nan welcome you aboard. Sail TUFF!

Vanity: *Captains Bob and Jan Robinson, Chef Jan Robinson*

VANITY is a luxurious 60' Motor Sailer. This owner-operated charter yacht is designed for privacy. Taking only four guests, VANITY assures you of individual consideration. Dine comfortably under the stars, enjoy international cuisine. Seven years of chartering give the Robinsons the knowledge of where the action is and where serenity prevails.

Verano Sin Final: *Captain Ted Dixon, Chef Jane Dixon*

"Verano Sin Final" is prehaps the best equipped Irwin 65' in the Virgin Islands. We take 8 guests and are fully equipped for scuba diving. We have 2 instructors and 1 dive master to show you the fabulous underwater world. Let Ted, Jane, Christine, and Andrew entertain you.

Victorious: *Captain John Barry, Chef Sheila Smith*

John has been sailing in the Caribbean for ten years. Sheila has spent the last three years running her own restaurant in Scotland. Victorious is a luxurious new cutom built Morgan 62' who sails beautifully. The combination of expert captaining, delicious cooking, and Victorious' spacious accommodation is unbeatable.

White Bay Sandcastle: *Captain Billy Hawkins and Chef Lisa Hawkins*
(formally of Yacht Ariguani)

Sandcastle is a small, personalized hotel for those who yearn to unwind. We cater to only a handful of guests and tranquility is our major attraction! Our comfortable cottages, superior cuisine, homespun hospitality and perfect white sand beach provide the ingredients for the most relaxing vacation you have ever had.

Wind's End: *Captain Jerry Dudley, Chef Jennifer Morden*

A 42' Endeavor built to accommodate 2-4 guests. A spacious, teak through-out interior, she's the perfect honeymoon yacht. Join us for a wonderful week aboard "Wind's End".

Winji: *Captain Rob Wilson, Chef Dorie Devnew*

Coming aboard WINJI, a beautiful 53' Pearson Ketch, you enter a world of luxury afloat. Chart your own course to a special, private vacation, custom tailored for one or two couples. Enjoy fine dining aboard in secluded anchorages. WINJI'S crew is ready to serve you.

COCKTAIL INDEX
(ALPHABETICAL ORDER)

*Indicates drinks that can be either alcoholic or non-alcoholic
+Indicates deliciously diet drinks

HORS D'OEUVRE INDEX

COCKTAIL INDEX

HORS D'OEUVRE INDEX

CHEESE

DIPS